CHICANO
BOUNTY HUNTER

Mike Quintana
Amit S.Katz

Disclaimer: The events depicted in this book are based on real events. Certain events and there location as well as individual's names and descriptions have been changed in order to protect their identity. Any apparent similarity to real persons (living or dead) or any events are entirely coincidental.

TABLE OF CONTENTS

PREFACE: RED CORNER BLUE CORNER

"And now, ladies and gentlemen for the main event of the evening, 10 rounds of boxing, standing on my right in the Blue Corner wearing red and black...."

Even if you are not a boxing fan, you have heard these words or some similar introduction like it before.
Probably from the lips of notable ring announcers such as Jimmy Lennon Jr or Michael Buffer, and chances are you didn't pay too much attention to the color of the corner the fighters were fighting out of.

Backstage all of the boxers fighting out of the Blue corner will be placed in one dressing room, and the same is true for the red corner. The "house" or the boxing organization putting on the show, have a vested interest in their prospect's winning.

The house will always place all of their fighters in one colored dressing room and often times, after the fights a specific colored backstage dressing room will contain either mostly winners or losers of the night's fights.

The Golden Boy fights at the Santa Ana Star Casino in Albuquerque, NM on April 28th 2012 were no exception.
The main event was a title fight that pitted Fidel Maldonado Jr and face of Golden Boy promotions in NM, against a little known underdog from Mexico by the name of Fernando Carcamo.

I was working the corner for Fernando's fight, but this time a lone fighter out of the roster of fighters hailing from the blue corner beat the house, with a 2nd round TKO.

We were booed walking to the ring, I was walking with my water bucket behind Fernando when one of the locals flipped me the bird at point blank range as yelled "You're going down Puto!!!"
The locals loved their home town hero, but once Fernando finished the fight the crowd changed their tune.

Leaving the ring, the team consisting of Fernando's coach, me and his manager were greeted with a warm pat on the back, smiles and Fernando even stayed ringside to sign autographs.

We made our way backstage, back to the blue corner dressing

room. Some of the fighters had already left while others were licking their wounds and wrapping their heads around their loss. Our team was elated, we walked into enemy territory and won. The other fighters in the dressing room and their team members were happy for us, in many ways they shared the underdog victory with us.

Mike was the manager for John Revish, a fighter from Baton Rouge. We spoke briefly during breakfasts at the hotel and at the press conference leading up to the fight.

In the blue dressing room after the fights he approached me, congratulated us on our victory and was genuinely happy for Fernando's victory.
Fernando had a sponsorship from the local paper in Obregon, Sonora. The paper made Team Carcamo baseball caps with their logo on them, which we wore into the ring.

Standing backstage all of a sudden Mike said "that's a nice baseball cap, can I have it"

I really didn't want to give him the cap so I said "you know what, I'll get your address and send you one" knowing very well that I wasn't going to send him anything, probably hoping he would just let it slide.

People are usually not confrontational, not without a reason. More times than not, if you give them an answer that is meant to brush them off, they'll take it, especially when it comes from a stranger.

But to my surprise Mike looked at me sideways and said "That's a lie, I will never see that baseball cap in the mail, will I?"

He was right, I wasn't going to send him shit and he knew it, but what surprised me was the speed at which he figured out that I was less than sincere, and then phrased it right back at me, sharp, clear and his delivery was not angry or sarcastic.

That's Mike in a nutshell, he knows people.

What I didn't know about Mike at the time, is that he has years of figuring out folks on the fly, his job requires that of him.

He has also learned to take into consideration the basic facts of a situation and figure out how an individual will react.

Our polite interaction backstage in the Blue dressing room after the fights, was just a taste of Mike's ability.

Since then, we have become good friends, and I'll often receive a call after midnight that finds me asleep in bed, from an ecstatic Mike riding an adrenaline high, followed by a funny bounty story well worth repeating.

1. THIS IS MIKE OR SAINTS DON'T BOUNTY HUNT

Everyone has heard sayings like "fight fire with fire" or "the best defense is an offense" and "Don't fry bacon naked" (you should disregard the last saying, please).

When you think about it, what these sayings really mean is that in order to execute any action which could be considered "pushing back", one needs a tool, a chemical reaction or a reaction of greater force than the one that brought about the current situation.

Take for example a dirty greasy stove hood, like the one you probably have in your kitchen.

For the last two years, you've enjoyed various foods which you cooked on the stove, whilst the fumes were being carried away through the vent above it.

But during that time you didn't run a finger over the hoods surface.

Then one day you do, and it's sticky, greasy, nasty and starting to give your whole house the smell that every meal prepared in your kitchen came out of a Mickey D's deep fat fryer.

In the name of "cleanliness" you say enough is enough, I can't ignore this any longer, and now you put some dish washing detergent in a glass with some water, and using a sponge with a little old fashioned elbow grease, attempt to remove the Exxon Valdez oil slick from your hood.

Well guess what? For all of your intents and purposes the soap ain't cutting through the grease, no matter how much good old fashion elbow grease you pour on this project.

What you are missing is the chemical force to break grease off of that surface.

Where Cascade has failed you, that balled gay nightclub bouncer Mr.Clean with Ammonia won't.

What you need in order to break down that grease once and for all is Ammonia.

A superior chemical force coupled with an action that can take care of the problem.

It's not really even fighting fire with fire, it is fighting fire with superior fire.

But all of this chemistry is occurring in the realm of the natural world, devoid of any human interaction.

Unencumbered by the forces of the world, a good man will more times than not, do good.

Once you start applying some pressure on him, some of it will penetrate and part of it will be deflected.

Apply enough pressure, enough life lessons, enough lessons born of street smarts and "The Good Man" will change.

Hopefully his heart will remain good at his core and hopefully his understanding of humans around him will become more realistic and not cynical.

But for the good man who has now evolved to understand human weakness, frailty, depravity and evil, something must be taken away.

The halo must be removed, and it's OK, that good man devoid of his halo can do the work, push back, be a tool in the hands of an essential chemical action which needs to occur but few are prepared to do.

We may throw money at him to do this job, we can also ridicule him for being lowly enough to engage in such a sleazy dirty profession for a buck, but that says nothing about his initial motivation to bounty hunt and it certainly does not show the proper respect.

Without this man, a simple crack head out on a $5000 bond, who chooses not to show up to court, may now be roaming the streets looking to get his fix and may break into your house or mug your grandmother.

Mike has no halo, he isn't missing it and certainly has no use for it, he needs a better Taser and a Sunday off.

If anything it would only get in the way of a swift morning nab of a fugitive.

Mike will fight with anyone, family, friends, strangers etc…anytime, over anything, when he is wrong and especially when he is right.

All the time he will enjoy every minute of that fight and never lose his cool, I am surprise he has never picked a fight with me, but then again he may just change his mind.

Mike is always respectful, a lot of yes sir and no ma'am, but like I said, don't piss him off unless you are just looking for a verbal altercation from a good hearted man who just doesn't give a shit.

He can often be found picking fights on Facebook with whole basketball and football teams by posting such comments as "Lakers you suck!!!" and "Raiders, you suck ass worse than the Lakers did last night!!!"

Don't be offended, Mike is at home laughing to himself or on the phone laughing about how you took offense to his Facebook post with me.

In the movie City Slickers, Curly dies in the middle of a cattle run. His long time team buddy "Cookie" is asked to eulogize him.

His parting words are "God I give you Curly, don't piss him off"

I should say that one day for Mike but I'll probably say "God, I give you my friend Bounty Mike, all good to the core and all rough on the outside, now can you please give him back his halo?"

2. BOUNTY HUNTING 101

We hear of bounty hunters and bail bondsman in everyday life, but most people are not quite sure how it all works.

So before we get into our book, we wanted to give the reader some of the basics of this part of the justice system.

Let's walk through a scenario to illustrate where a bounty hunter comes into the picture.

An individual in the US is considered innocent until proven guilty, but if they are arrested and a judge deems that there is a strong chance that the defendant may be a risk to society, he will only allow them back on the streets if he can guarantee that they will show up to court.

The system also recognizes that an individual who is arrested for breaking the law, still has bills to pay or a family to feed and or responsibilities elsewhere in life, and therefore will want to allow them to go back to their lives until they are required to show up in court.

In order to insure this individual's return to court a monetary fee is demanded of them, this is called a Bond, meaning a monetary demand binding them to comply with the courts requests of appearance.

Let's say you are arrested and at your arraignment before a Judge, he determines that your Bond amount is $50,000.
You now have two options;

1. Pay the $50,000 which you will eventually get back, it may be 12 months, 2 years etc…depending upon when all the legalities finally end, or
2. Contact a Bail Bondsman to put up the $50,000 for you if you cannot afford it.

Most people can't afford to have $50,000 of their money sitting for an indefinite amount of time in the hands of the court, as well as the fact that most people simply don't have an extra $50,000 lying around to begin with.

In order to use the services of the Bondsman, they will ask you to pay a certain percent of the bond or Guarantee that amount in property as collateral.

That percent of the bond or fee is nonrefundable, it should be considered the price you will have to pay in order to use the services of the bondsman.

If you don't have this fee or equal value in property, a family member or a friend can cosign for you, but that means that now their property and or money are being used and they will be held financially responsible for your behavior.

If the defendant is a responsible individual, great, no problem, but if they are not, the cosigner may be looking at the possibility of losing their collateral, Ouch!!!

So be careful when you cosign a bond for anyone including a family member. Sometimes bailing a family member out will not serve their best interests and only hurt you financially and inevitably damage the relationship.

Should the individual that has posted bail show up to court and comply at all times with the courts requests to show up, all is good in the world.

But should they forget to appear or skip a court appearance, the court will go back to the bondsman and he will attempt to figure out why you did not show up to court.

It's still not the end of the world, it merely means that you have one less chance to be responsible, and the bondsman will probably call your house, your friends, the cosigner of the bond etc…all in an attempt to get you back to court.

But if at this point you do not comply, your whereabouts are unknown, or you refuse for whatever reason to show up to court, the bondsman will activate a bounty hunter to find you in order to get you back to court.

This can be done through the use of force, a bounty hunter makes his living catching fugitives, if he doesn't catch his fugitive he won't make a living.

Think about the last statement like this, a Police man gets paid for a job whether he is successful or not, a bounty hunter only gets paid for a successful catch of a fugitive, who is more motivated to catch a bail jumper? Get the picture?

Once the Bounty Hunter catches you, he will take you to Jail. Now that you are in the hands of the law, it is now out of the bounty

5

hunter and bail bondsman's hands, and it is law enforcement that will insure your appearance before a judge.

At this point the bounty hunter will return to the bondsman and get paid for catching you and returning you to the system.

But now it is also up to the bondsman to collect any collateral for the bounty activity, which can mean the loss of any property placed as collateral such as a car or a house, once again, ouch!!!

The moral of the story is, comply with the courts, if you get into trouble with the law and can't afford to post bail I hope you have good family members and friends, and if you did something really bad and decide that it is better to run than to face the law, I hope your family and friends will be understanding enough when they lose their collateral, and lastly, make sure you run far away, quickly and that you are never seen again or else...

3. THE ONE THAT GOT AWAY

No one has ever got away*

*If I didn't get them the cops did.

4. DANCING WITH SUNSHINE

Most people grow up idolizing someone famous, an actor, an athlete, a rock star, or an historical figure like Abraham Lincoln.

Mikes childhood hero was an obscure pop culture figure, who came by the house when he was growing up as a 10 year old kid living in Riverside CA. by the name of William "Tiny" Boyles.

Tiny was a friend of the family, he stood 6ft 8, weigh 386lb, had a beard, wore a cowboy hat, and to little 10 year old Mike seemed like and indestructible super hero.

If the truth be told, Tiny seemed like an indestructible super hero to normal adults, you couldn't help but notice him and you knew this giant had a story, which was all true.

Tiny was the first real life pop culture Bounty Hunter, by 1981 he had published several books about his notorious bounty hunting exploits, was making TV appearances and being courted by Hollywood.

Mike "My whole life, I always wanted to bounty hunt, it took me a while to get into it, but I never stopped wanting to do it since talking to Tiny when I was a kid".

I finished bounty hunting training and certification back in the mid 2000's.

The first thing I did was approach Jason Ramirez, out of Kings Bonds in Denver.

He sized me up and probably didn't think much of me, so he gave me the hardest bond he had, a $10,000 No Hold Bond for a coke dealer out of Commerce City by the name of Sunshine Flores.

I got the bond in the summer, I was managing fighters and working some construction at the time, but I knew I had to start somewhere and I hit the ground running.

I spent any extra time I had hunting down leads and figuring out who Sunshine was and where I could find her.

The problem I was having at the time, was that I had no existing contact structure that could lead me to her, everything was new, and it took me a few months to set up my network.

But I was constantly getting closer and closer, and I knew it was just a matter of time before a good lead appeared.

In this case it wasn't one lead, but several indicators that led to a trailer in Commerce City, often used by crack and meth heads.

All of Sunshine's mail was being directed to this one trailer, good enough a place to start zeroing in on her movements.

It was now November, Colorado got hit early by a Blizzard and Commerce was blanketed with ice and snow.

I was a little nervous but I just walked up to the door, and knocked on it.

When the door opened I was greeted by the powerful fumes of meth being cooked inside, as well as a real thin and gaunt looking guy in his early 30's, but from the amount of meth he'd been doing he looked more like the crypt keeper.

Mike "do you know where I can find Sunshine"

Meth Head "Who?"

Mike "Sunshine Flores, all of her mail arrives at this location"

Meth Head "Naaaa…don't know her"

Mike "From the smell of things I have enough to put this trailer on wheels and confiscate all of its contents, but if you help me find Sunshine I'll look the other way"

Meth Head "Fuck off"

He shut the door, allowing my eyeballs to finally recover from the chemical assault they were being subjected to, man did I need some Visine.

My good friend Jerry had a long bed tow truck, and I decided to give him a call, he was just getting back to the shop when I reached him, and he headed on out to Commerce to help me apply some needed "Psychological pressure" on Mr. less than cooperative Trailer park Meth Head.

Jerry pulled the tow truck up to the trailer and went about setting the trailer up to be taken away.

As we are preparing the "phony tow", Mr. Meth Head pops his head out of the door, takes one look at us, steps outside, shuts the door and runs up to me.

He started begging me not to take his Trailer, I told him there is only one way that was going to happen and that was if he connected me with Sunshine.

9

So he gave me her number and I said goodbye to Jerry and Mr. Meth Head who seemed to have a much relieved look on his face, while I sported a devilish smile on mine.

I was getting closer, I called the number, first time no answer, second time no answer, third time bingo, a female voice on the other line said "Do I know you?"

Mike "My name is Jessie, you don't know me, a guy by the name of James turned me on to you."
(James was a made up name, luckily she knew a contact guy at a bar she hustled out of, by the name of James).

Sunshine "OK, James, cool"

Mike "I need two T-Shirts" (Code for two x $2000 bags of Coke)

Sunshine "Where are you?"

Mike "By the trailer in Commerce"

Sunshine "How do you know about the trailer? Are you some fucking cop?"

Mike "No, I ain't no cop, James told me, remember?"

Sunshine "I'll be there in an hour"

An hour goes by, two hours go by, three hours go by, four hours go by and no Sunshine, so I call her again.

Mike "Are you coming?"

Sunshine "Do you have the money?"

Mike "Yes, when will you be here? This isn't for me, it's for friends and if you can't make it, I've got to move on to someone who can get me the two T-Shirts I need"

Sunshine "I'll be there in 20 minutes"

The 20 minutes turned into another hour, no one ever said drug dealers are punctual individuals.

The time was approximately 9pm when a Blazer pulled up outside of the trailer, with two guys in the front and out of the back popped little 5ft 5 120lb, 23 year old Sunshine, blondish brown hair, beautiful hazel eyes, really cute, wearing a large bomber jacket probably two or three sizes larger than she needed.

If you saw Sunshine in public, you would have never guessed a girl this cute was in the drug dealing business.

She walked right up to me and motioned me to follow her into the trailer.

I was starting to get worried, what if Mr. Meth Head says something?

He's a druggy, not too bright and he could pop off, no time to worry, it's about to all happen right now.

We stepped into the entry of the trailer, there were 3 guys including Mr. Meth head and 2 gals, stoned out of their minds lying on the floor and beat up furniture, they didn't say a word and Sunshine lead the way into an empty back room.

She turned to me and said "where's the money?"

My palms were sweating inside my jacket, the adrenaline was coursing through my body, my heart was beating fast and I was trying to keep a lid on my nervousness.

All day long I knew there was a strong possibility that this moment was coming, I ran the scenario in my mind over and over again. She was going to ask for the dough and I was going to whip out my cuffs, grab an arm and cuff it, but I wasn't sure about what was going to happen next.

In one lightning fast and fluid motion, I pulled out the cuffs, grabbed a wrist and click, one wrist was mine.

Sunshine went nuts, and it was on, she became the love child of the Warner Brothers Tasmanian devil and a whirling dervish with MMA skills.

She probably did a little bump of her own product before making it out to the trailer, the girl was strong, much stronger than her appearance.

She fought like a man, bobbing, weaving, punching, tugging on the cuffs, anything to get away, all the while screaming "you mother fucker" but I had this little tornado lassoed and I wasn't letting go.

From the force of all the back and forth tugging and pulling, we both lost balance and hit the floor.

The two bags of cocaine must have been taped to her body and when she went down chest first they exploded on impact, spreading a Colombian dust cloud of coke all over everything, the floor, her clothes, her hair, my clothes etc.

At the same time the coke was being crop dusted across the room, a 357 Magnum popped out of her oversized bomber jacket and now she was attempting to reach it.

This gave me an opportunity to place all of my weight on her back, crank her right hand cuffed wrist behind her and pull it up towards the back of her head, inflicting severe pain.

I shouted "Put your left hand behind your back" all the while applying steady and forceful pressure to her right cuffed wrist. She finally gave in, up and over went the left wrist and I cuffed it. She was mine, I got her to her feet and we headed past the 5 stoners and out the trailer door.

The two guys in the Blazer took one look at us and floored it out of the trailer park, leaving their drug dealer boss behind.

Commerce City is in Adams County, but the bond was from Jefferson County.

I called the local police and told them about the lose 357 in the back of the trailer and the coke.

I then headed for Jefferson County Jail, because even though Adams County Jail would have transported her to Jefferson within a week, I wanted to expedite everything and above all, I wanted to get paid for my efforts as fast as I could.

When we were finally on our way I could hear the sound of laughter coming from Sunshine, I had her in cuffs and she was laughing?

Mike "What's so funny?

Sunshine "I've been running for a long time, do you know who I am?"

I thought she was going to tell me that her coke money would get her back on to the streets by tomorrow, I knew this wasn't going to happen, so I just listened.

Sunshine "I am one of the biggest drug dealers in Commerce, and you caught me slipping, props to you Jessie if that's even your real name, are you a detective?"

Mike "No ma'am, I'm a bounty hunter"

Sunshine "A fucking bounty hunter!!! I can't believe that a fucking bounty hunter was the one that finally caught me, you know I'm going a way for a while"

Mike "Yes ma'am"

The next day I called Jason's office and said "You know that bounty you gave me back in July, the bitch is in custody"

Jason "Are you kidding me? 3 other bounty hunters have been looking for this girl for over 10 months and gave up, come down to my office tomorrow and I'll cut you a check.

Mike "Yes Sir"

Judging by just how surprised Jason was about the news, it seemed that his perception of me changed in an instant. I couldn't wait for tomorrow's payday and the next bond Jason was going to have for me.

5. THERE IS NO PLACE LIKE HOME

It was Friday afternoon, my phone rings and it's Mike, not the usual time to hear from him, but it's got to be good.

Mike "Hey, what are you doing?" Classic Mike, he always starts off like that.

Me "Nothing, what's up?"

Mike "Man, these bondsmen, I'm telling you, why do they always call me after their cheap fuck ups mess things up?" Mike sounded upbeat, even though the words were words of frustration.

Me "Because they know you can fix their problem?"

Mike "Ya, I know, but why don't they just call me first?"

Me "Because they're cheap?"

Mike "Exactly! Thank you, Cheap and then it ends up costing them more and cutting into their profit which keeps them thinking cheap, when all they needed to do was call me in the first place"

Me "But Mike, you're Mexican, you already do the same job cheaper than a white guy or a black guy, how much cheaper can you do this gig?" I'm probably the only person in the universe who can pop off like that to Mike.

Mike "Ha Ha Ha...Very funny.

Me "What happened Mike"

Mike "There's this hooker out on a $2500 bond, this bondsman tells me this guy Chuck, who by the way I introduced to this bondsman, has screwed this bust up three times and she's still out on the streets.
The bondsman was behaving all weird, I asked him a few questions and found out that Chucky had been talking smack about me, how I wasn't any good and stuff.

But when 5ft 2" Charley came back empty handed 3 times, he finally called me.

I get the feeling Chucky ain't getting anymore work from this bondsman.

To make a long story short, I tell him I'll have her in Adams County Jail before noon, he tells me if I can do that he will give me twice the bounty, meaning I'll pull down $500.

 So you know what I do, I drive to her mother's house, ya! guess

14

who cosigned for her?

I Park the car outside and call her on my cell phone.
She answers the phone and tells me she is in Cheyenne Wyoming.
Far be it from me to understand the migratory patterns of the Semi domesticated North American Homo Sapiens Sapiens Prostitutes Padonka Donkus Maximus aka Fat Ass Hoe.

Now Cheyenne is right across the state line, and maybe the hooking is good there, but I knew she was at moms.

As my luck would have it, mid conversation, the door opens and Dakota Harris aka Cherry Diamond steps outside and starts walking towards my vehicle.

She passes me all the while talking with me on her cell phone.

When she was about 20 feet from my car, I step out of my vehicle and say into my cell phone "turn around".

Low and behold, there I am larger than life, handcuffs in hand with a big grin on my face.

Cherry "Oh...Mike...I just got back from Cheyenne...uh..."

Mike "How did you do that? Did you call the Enterprise? Did you say beam me up Scotty or did you tap your red shoes together and say There is no place like home Dorothy?"

Sometimes shame is a real powerful tool, you don't always get it during a bust, but Cherry had plenty of it when I straight up caught her bullshitting me.

She was blushing, which is something I never thought I would cause a hooker to do, and for that one maybe I should have had a swelling of pride.

I asked her to turn around, she wasn't putting up any resistance, on went the cuffs and I ran her down to the Jail, snapped a picture of her, called the bondsman up and told him she's in the clink.
I posted the picture of her on my Facebook page and sent him a picture as well.

Now I'm up an extra $250, which has cut into his profit, but do you think in the future he's going to call me first? Why don't they ever learn?

I hate to brag man, but I'm good at getting these fugitives, that $500 was taking candy from a baby.

Me "Where are you now?"

Mike "I'm heading down to the bondsman's office right now, we still need to work out the whole chucky fiasco. He also said he has two $10,000 bonds for me.

Me "So maybe your performance today got a little "cheap" out of his system?"

Mike "You know, you're right! He did just sweeten up" Mike sounded surprised.

Me "Isn't that how it usually works? The haters come around sooner or later"

Mike "Naaaa…haters just keep on hating, fuck 'em.

6. AND TO MAKE MATTERS WORSE...

I was supposed to talk to Mike last night about another bounty story.

I called him at 5pm, but he was at Sloane Boxing Gym working with the amateur fighters.

He said he'd call me back at 6pm California time so I waited. It was 6:30 when I decided to call him, I figured he would answer.

The phone rang but went straight to voice mail so I decided to call again.

This time his wife answered, she said he was busy talking to a "guy" which means "fugitive" or someone connected to a bounty.

I told Sonya to let him know that I was looking for him and to remind him about a certain story he told me. She promised to let him know.

It was getting late and I didn't hear back from Mike so I just went to bed and didn't think anything of it.

At 8am I was still in bed when my cell rang, it was Mike, I could tell from the sound of his voice he was riding another one of his bounty rush highs.

Mike "Hey Amit, are you up?"

Me "I am now, did you get my message last night from the misses?"

Mike "Ya, I did, but I was crazy busy man, it was like the Wild West here last night and all morning"

Me "What's going on?"

Mike "After I got back from the gym I got a call from the cousin of this 24 year old girl I've been chasing for some drug offense. He tells me she is about to head on over to a friend's house, but he wasn't sure and the moment he knew anything he would call me, so I had to stay in chase mode.

Then I got a similar call for this other guy who has been bull shitting me about turning himself in, so I was now in double chase mode.

So I am sitting around, wound up, ready to pounce but nothing is happening.

I decide to go to bed, figuring that the red alert was over and that I'd pick it all up tomorrow.

17

But I couldn't sleep, at 3 am I get up, get dressed and head out to catch these punks.

As I am getting in my car I get a call from Uncle Ramsey and bond cosigner for his nephew 23 year old Anthony, who skipped a court appearance for some peeping Tom charges, so now this is fugitive number three who is on my radar all of a sudden.

He tells me Anthony is at his mom's house right now and that if I head over there I could pick him up.

I head on over to the house, but before I got there I called the Denver Sheriff's Department and ask for back up on a house search of Anthony's mom's place.

In this job you have to take into consideration who you are chasing.

A peeping tom is by definition crafty and sneaky, the fact that he's 23 means that he will be quick, couple these with the fact that he doesn't work, has no income and he's on the run all mean one thing, If I roll up on mom's house in the early morning, the fact that she is aiding and abetting a fugitive of the law will be no deterrent, she will stall me long enough for him to slip away.

It is now 5:45am, I meet the sheriff's cruiser a block away and ask them to accompany me to the front door.

Mom opens up the door but it is latched by a chain.

Mike "Where is Anthony?"

Mom "He's not hear"

Mike "In that case let me in so that I can look around, verify that he's not on your premises and I will leave you alone"

Mom "Go away, I am not letting you in to search anything, I have rights"

Mike "I am here with the Sheriff's Department, officer please tell her what rights she has"

The officer walked up from behind me to the open latch crack of door, where the mom's face was just poking out.

Officer "Ma'am, This Bail Enforcement Agent has the right to enter your premises and look around, I suggest you open the door and let us in"

Mom "None of you have the right to force your way onto my property, go away"

18

Mike "Please open the door, I promise it will be quick and we won't disturb your property or your belongings if you just cooperate.

The mom just shut the door and there was some sound of commotion inside the house, which went on for a few minutes.

I was losing my patients, I also didn't want to have to go looking for that skinny punk in the rafters with all the fiberglass insulation, which itches like fuck when you scrape up against it.

Mike "This is your last warning, let me in or I will be forced to kick down this door" No answer, she was not helping matters.

Mike "On a count of three I suggest you step back because I will be kicking this door in, one, two, and three"

My right foot hit that sucker with all the force of a Kansas City Twister, the poor door did not stand a chance, it busted at the lock and flew right open, Score: Mike 1, Moms Door a big fat Zero.

Now I moved quickly, mom was shouting, screaming, cussing and coming at me but the officers blocked her path.

I went into the first room, over turned the bed, looked through the closets, in the bathroom, then moved to the second room, turned it upside down but no Peeping Tom Boy.

Kitchen pantry was empty and laundry room too, where was this little punk?

I stepped back into the living room, her other son an 8 years old was sitting in the middle of a large couch, looking a little upset.

The couch looked a little high off the ground as if maybe just maybe mom had tucked Anthony under it and placed her other son on top in order to create a perfect "hidden in plane site" effect.
I turned to the kid and said "hey kid, what's your name?"
"Eric" he replied.
"Hey Eric, why don't you go stand by your mom I need to look over there" and pointed in the direction of the TV and couch set.

Little Eric got up walked over and stood by his mom who was standing by the officers.

I walked over the strange looking couch, the mom lurched forward and let out a "don't do that…"

I flipped the couch over and…nothing, nada, a big fat goose egg. Anthony wasn't in the house after all, and to make matters worse his nutty mother could have avoided her busted door if she had only let us in.

If I am forced to kick down a door of a house, it doesn't matter if the fugitive is there or not, the fact that I was forced to do it places liability on the house owner and not me.

Why she behaved like that is beyond me, just let me in and I'll be on my way.

Mike "Hey Amit, hold on the line one minute, I have a call from the officer on my private line, just be quite, I'll put it on the loud speaker and you can tune into the whole conversation, hold on…" Mike put me on hold and answered his private phone.

Mike "Hello"

Officer "Quintana, were you able to locate Anthony after we left this morning"

Mike "No, but I am heading over to a bus stop a few miles from here to see if I can find him outside of his friend's house, he's not getting away"

Officer "good, he has another 5 warrants out for pretty much the same violations"

Mike "Really! He's a peeping pro. I'll be sure to call you as soon as I have him"

Officer "If we find him I will let you know, by the way, any Idea why his mom wouldn't let us in, even though we were there?"

Mike "No idea, I'm about to call her brother, he's the cosigner on this bond"

Officer "Keep up the good work"

Mike "Thanks". Mike hung up with the officer and picked up his personal phone.

Mike "Could you catch that"

Me "I sure did"

Mike "Speak of the devil, its Uncle Ramsey, I'll put the phone of the loud speaker again, check it out"

Mike picked up the business line and said "Hello"

Ramsey "Hi Quintana, I hear you were over at my sister's house, no Anthony?"

Mike "No sir, but don't worry, I'll catch that little punk nephew of yours, don't you worry"

Ramsey "I hope you do, I heard she wouldn't let you in and you had to kick the door down"

Mike "Yes sir, I don't know why she didn't open up and let us in, now she's got to pay to fix the door"

Ramsey "She's making things worse, please catch this boy before there is any more trouble"

Mike "I will, soon"

Mike picked up his private cell phone and said "did you catch that?"

Me "Yes I did, I thought you may have been pumping the story up a bit"

Mike "Now you know, thank you". Mike was starting to sound tired, he'd been up since the early morning on three cases and no one had been caught yet, in spite of doors being kicked in, sheriff's being called and dimes being dropped on these fugitives.

Me "What are you going to do now?"

Mike "I think I'll go home, get some rest and wait"

Me "Good idea, get some rest, they'll still be there when you get up". I got a call from Mike at 9pm the following day.

Mike "Amit, guess what?" Mike sounded really happy.

Me "Oh, Hi Mike, good to hear your voice too"

Mike "Oh Ya, Hey Buddy, how are you?"

Me "I'm good, now what are you so happy about?"

Mike "After I got off the phone with you I got a call from a friend of Anthony's. I had been talking to him for a while, took a little bit of convincing, but you know me I have the gift of the gab and I was able to convince him to help me.

He set Anthony up, offering him a place to stay and promising to lend him some money. I got there around 9pm and hid in the other room.

Anthony showed up and while they were talking in the living room I came up from behind, surprised him got him on the floor, cuffed him and off we went to Jail, one down two to go.

As I was pulling away from the jail the second fugitive, the guy who was stalling me over turning himself in calls me.

He finally came to his senses and wanted me to pick him up, so I headed over to his girlfriend's house and took him in.

21

I had no peace over these cases because of their urgent nature, and now they were folding one by one.

By the time I had locked the second fugitive up it was already almost 12pm so I headed home and went to bed.

My phone rang at 6am, it was the cousin of the 24 year old drug fugitive, she told me her cousin was doped up and asleep on the couch at her house and all I needed to do was come and pick her up.

I figured things were going my way, so I didn't even shower, I just put on some clothes and rushed out the door.

Sure enough stoned sleeping beauty was on the couch, she was so out of it she didn't even wake up when I slipped the cuffs on her.

Me "That's great, you got all three in less than 24 hours and they were super easy"

Mike "It's never this easy, but sometimes it's nice not to dance that hard for your supper".

7. TWEEDLEDEE AND TWEEDLE DUMBASS

Its 10am on Tuesday morning, my cell phone rings, I look at the led and the familiar red Quintana Boxing logo pops up, its Mike.

Me "Mike, what's up? Everything OK?"

Mike "Hey Amit, I wanted to touch base with you before I leave for West Virginia"

Me "What's in West Virginia? Do you have a fighter joining the Chitlin' Circuit?" (For those who are unfamiliar with boxing, the Chitlin' Circuit is the name given to a series of lower level boxing shows held on the west coast, mainly in the South).

Mike "Chitlin' Circuit? Ha ha ha…." Mike erupted into his great laugh, when you hear that laugh you can't help but join in and I was laughing along for a second.

Mike "No Chitlin Circuit for my fighters, I'm off to catch a fugitive"

Me "But Mike, aren't you only licensed in Colorado? And why are you going so far to catch this one?"

Mike "I'm licensed to catch a fugitive period, and I'm going to get this one, oh man am I going to get her, especially after the weekend I had" He sounded like someone had double dared him.

Me "What happened over the weekend?"

Mike "I got a $10,000 bounty for this little crack head in Westminster called Lisa Bishop, 5ft 4" white girl, blue eyes blond hair, maybe a buck ten soaking wet.

It was supposed to be an easy catch, I do these all the time, a little crack or meth head gets busted, a family member gets a bondsman to post bail, and they hit the streets and go missing, why? Because they're addicts.

We try to get them back over the phone, but they don't want to go to jail and deal with the withdrawal or the consequences, so they run, and then it's CBH all the way.

The parents posted Lisa's bail and I had their address, so on Saturday around 9am I was already parked outside the house casing the place.

The neighborhood was a really nice one, the houses were really well kept, not what you'd usually expect from a drug offender.

23

But this is what happens when your kid goes down the crack Hwy, and it doesn't matter from what neighborhood they come from or how much money their parents have.

I noticed that there was a brick wall around the property and a really sweet looking trailer in the back.

Lisa was either in the house or in that trailer, I just knew it.

The moment I got out of my vehicle, the front door of the house opened and a man stepped out.

He was in his early 60's, full head of gray hair, dressed in Jeans and a blue jacket.

He walked right up to me "Good morning, who are you visiting in this neighborhood?" It was Lisa's father Marvin, he was the one that signed the bond, the bondsman had tried to talk with him about getting Lisa back, but he claimed he didn't know his daughters whereabouts.

Mike "What business is it of yours?"

Marvin "I am the head of this neighborhoods watch, if you have business here then I suggest you go about it, or please leave"
Papa Marvin was rude to say the least, wouldn't you say?
Mike "When I am good and ready to leave this neighborhood I will do so"

Marvin Bishop turned, walked back to the house and shut the door, but no sooner had he closed the door, the blinds in the front windows got drawn shut.

I could see from the right hand corner of the blinds a little gap that was being held open, I got back into my vehicle and looked at the gap with my binoculars, it was Marvin and he was looking back at me with his binoculars.

It was clear now, they were hiding Lisa and now they knew I was the one who was looking for her.

Marvin was either paranoid, had some serious veterans post-traumatic stress disorder, was intent on keeping his daughter out of jail or all of the above.

Fathers have a special bond with their daughters, I get it, but this wasn't going to help daddy's little girl at all.

I could have called the Westminster Police and request that they accompany me to the door, then asked Mr. Bishop to allow me to

24

search the house, but for some reason I just sat and waited.

Maybe I was waiting for the morning coffee to kick in, or maybe it was the whole father daughter relationship that made me just take it easy for a few minutes.

I had been in my vehicle for no more than 20 minutes, when I saw the Mom walk out of the back door of the house towards the trailer parked in the back yard.

Mom was a little heavy set, but her daughter shared many of her features.

She walked with her arms crossed as If she was holding something, and a little hunched over as if shielding it from the elements, she opened the door and shut it behind her.

I kept my binoculars fixed on the trailer, if I've said it once I've said it a million times, bounty hunting is also a waiting game.

Mom had been in the trailer for about 25 minutes, I was darting back and forth from the front door and its adjacent window accompanied by Marvin's watchful gaze, to the trailer in the back.

All of a sudden the trailer door opened, mom started walking towards the back of the property, but there was something different about her, she wasn't heavy set anymore.

Hold on! That wasn't mom at all, it was Lisa, she had swapped clothes with mom.

Lisa was now bolting towards the properties back wall, she leaped over the wall cowboy style and disappeared in the alley behind the house.

I turned the key, swung the wheel hard to my left and hit the gas, steering the car towards the alley.

When I turned into the alley I could see little Lisa running, she was trying to make it out of the alley and into the busy road away from the house.

Lisa was fast but not fast enough, and I pulled up beside her, opened the window and shouted "Stop running" but Lisa wasn't stopping for anything.

I repeated my demand several times with urgency, but Lisa didn't even as much as turn her head and look at me, she had a scared and frantic look on her face.

I opened the car door, increased the cars speed and whack, hit Lisa

25

from behind sending her forwards crashing to the concrete.

I passed Lisa and brought my car to a stop about 10 feet away from where she had hit the ground.

Lisa was up and running by the time I darted out of my vehicle, cuffs in hand, ready to pounce on this little rabbit.

She must have been a track and field athlete in high school, possibly a hurdler, because she leaped over a chain blocking the parking access to a neighbor's car port, and was now heading towards the front.

I got back into my car, thinking I could catch her in the front yard if I drove around the block, but when I got there, she was nowhere to be found.

I drove around the neighborhood houses looking for any signs of a mad dashing Lisa, but there was no movement, the rabbit had gotten away, Damn!!! Just a few hours earlier this appeared to be an easy catch.

I circled for about an hour but I couldn't find her, so I went back to the house and looked at the front and the trailer through my binoculars, but there was no movement. This storm came up quick and died down without a trace of Lisa.

Then my phone rang, I answered it, but it was Luanne the girlfriend of another fugitive I had been chasing.

I spoke to her a couple of days earlier, she promised to give me a call when her boyfriend Nick came over to hide out, I guess the love faded the moment she found out that her prince in shining armor was a little punk drug dealer.

There is no better way to say "the love is gone baby" than to do it with an arrest from yours truly.

Luanne left the door open, Nick was asleep on the couch, all I had to do was roll up, walk in and grab his sorry ass in his sleep, easy money.

So I let Lisa run for now, and headed over to Luanne's, where sure enough, would be Carlos Escobar was pushing up Z's, boy did he have a rude awakening.

Once I had Nick locked up in Adams county Jail, I returned to look for Lisa, It was about 6pm and it was getting dark.

There was no light coming from the house or the trailer in the back.

I decided to sit and wait it out and I was there until 12pm, but nothing was moving.

It appeared as if the Bishops knew that this location was now too hot and went to a friend's house, or a family member.

I was left with no choice but to abandon the chase for the evening and get some well needed rest.

I woke up Tuesday morning, ready to resume my chase and headed out to the Bishop residence.

I pulled up to the house and went looking for any signs of life.

The house was dark, the trailer was locked, there was a paper on the front porch. All the signs were telling me that no one had been here since yesterday.

Just as a bit of frustration was setting in when I saw a neighbor come out of the house across the street, she was an old lady in her 80's, I walked up to her and started a conversation.

Mike "Good morning ma'am, have you see the Bishops this morning?

Neighbor "No, they left yesterday afternoon" The kind old lady had a gentle and soft hi pitched voice, I could tell she was telling the truth.

Mike "Did they say where they were going?"

Neighbor "They always go to visit family back home on the east coast, they've been doing it for years"

Mike "Where is home on the east coast?"

Neighbor "Rhodell West Virginia" WTF!!! Rhodell? I never heard of the place.

I called my bondsman Jason and told him about the situation, Lisa was getting to be a more difficult bounty by the minute.

Mike "Lisa Bishop is in Rhodell, West Virginia"

Jason "Where the fuck is Rhodell?"

Mike "I don't know? Who the hell knows? Can you do me a favor and look this place up on Wikipedia, I'll hang on the line while you do it" I could hear Jason rattling on his computer in the office.

Jason "It's a little town, population no more than a few hundred folks, Mike, I want you to go get her, I'm not taking another total loss on this one"

Mike "West Virginia? OK, but you've got to sweeten the deal"

Jason "I'll give you $5000"

Mike "I make that in 2 days and I won't even leave the greater Denver area, you've got to do better than that" I knew he was low balling it.

Jason "OK, $8500 but you've got to leave today"

Mike "OK, I'm on it, I'll have her back in 4 days"

This was a long way to go for a fugitive, but somehow I have faced more difficult bounties with more dangerous fugitives and I couldn't let this one get away.

I went home, packed my bag, said good bye to the misses and called you to let you know I'll be gone for about 4 days"

Me "Are you sure she's in West Virginia Mike? What if the old lady got it wrong?"

Mike "She was the type to tell the complete truth, a neighborhood gossip, Lisa is where the old lady said she would be, I know it"

Me "OK, be safe, you're going out of your element"

Mike "When do I ever go bounty hunting in my back yard?"

Me "You know what I mean buddy"

Mike "Ya, I know, I'll be fine, I'll call you when I get back"

It was now Friday and no message from Mike, Saturday rolled around and at about 2pm my phone rang and it was Mike.

Me "Mike, how are you? Are you back in Colorado?"

Mike "Yup, I'm home, let me fill you in, you will not believe what I am about to tell you"

I got on the 70 freeway heading east, it took me about a day and a half to get to Charleston, West Virginia.

When I got there I decided to call the local Sheriff's Department in Rhodell, let them know that I was coming in heading south on the 64, get directions to the station, and inform them of the nature of my visit.

I asked the dispatcher to connect me with the officer in charge, and I was connected within no more than 60 seconds with Officer Courtney.

He spoke with a real twang of a southern accent, was polite and promised to help me apprehend my fugitive.

This was refreshing, I usually get help from the local departments back home, but no one is ever this eager to help.)

I told Officer Courtney to expect me at around 8pm, but I pulled into the station at 7:45pm

There were 5 officers on duty, all polite and much like their station commander Officer Courtney, were happy to see me and eager to help.

I was starting to get a little freaked out by this southern hospitality, I have never met cops who were this chipper about meeting a bounty hunter.

In fact, they informed me that they don't get a lot of bounties in their town and they just wanted to help me get this fugitive, as well as rid their little town of this unwanted element.

Mike "Officer Courtney, since this town is so small, maybe you know the family of the fugitive?"

Officer Courtney "We know everyone in these parts, what's the fugitive's name?"

Mike "Lisa Bishop"

Officer Courtney turned to his other men on duty and asked "Anyone know the whereabouts of the Bishop kid?"

One of the officers said "yes, she got a job today at the warehouse" The officers name tag said Mack.

Mike "Can you accompany me to the factory tomorrow morning?"

Officer Mack "I can do better than that, we will accompany you tomorrow morning to the apartment complex, where she is renting a 1 bed room". This was getting creepier by the minute, Lisa had only been in town for maybe a day, how did they know so much about her whereabouts and what she was up to?

Mike "Officer Mack, How do you know so much about where she works and where she is staying?"

Officer Mack "My Auntie owns the factory and my wife's cousin owns the apartment complex" Yup, it was pretty country creepy, but it was breaking my way, and anyway who am I to question good old fashion luck.

Mike "Does anyone's family own a motel near here, where I can get a place to sleep for a few hours?"

Officer Courtney "The nearest place is a motel 6 off Hwy 77"

29

We agreed to meet back up at the station, bright and early at 7:30am.

I got to my room around 10pm and just crashed, tomorrow and the next few days were going to be long.

My cell phone alarm went off at 6:30am, if it had gone off at 12 noon it would have still been too early, man was I tired, but nothing some breakfast and 2 cups of coffee wouldn't fix.

I showed up at the station as promised, Thursday 7:30am sharp. When I walked in all 5 men were there just as I left them the night before.

None of them were yawning or looked tired, and their uniforms looked clean and freshly pressed, now I was really getting freaked out. How were they so fresh?

Was it some country food ingredient in their grits? A higher percent of moonshine in their diet? Clean stress free living? A genetic mutation from generations of coal mining? Or maybe I had seen one too many Twilight Zone episodes.

Either way, they were ready to go and all 5 officers were coming along.

I would have been happy with just one, but this was about as much action as they had seen in a while.

Officer Mack led the way in his cruiser, followed by Officer Courtney and then me in my vehicle.

We parked outside the apartment complex, as quietly and discreetly as possible.

Officer Mack's wife's cousin met us outside the place, and just pointed to a second story condo at the eastern part of the complex and just said "Number 209".

The officers took my lead, I told two of them to head to the back of the condo and wait underneath the balcony in case track star girl decided to pole vault off, run a 10K and go for a gold medal in the decathlon.

I headed towards the front door followed by Officer Courtney, Mack and a third officer.

I wasted no time and banged on the door "Lisa, I know you're in there, open up"

The door to Lisa's apartment was so flimsy that I could hear her and another person talking.

A male voice shouted behind the door "Who is this?"

Mike "Colorado Bounty Hunters, I'm here for Lisa Bishop, open the door now"

The male voice replied "There is no Lisa here, you have the wrong apartment" now I had a little doubt running through my head, did the old lady across the street make a mistake with the town's name in West Virginia? Did Officer Mack have the right girl or maybe his wife's cousin gave us the wrong apartment?

I looked at Officer Mack whilst simultaneously bending my elbows, lifting my hands and turning them up to face the sky, a gesture that said "Are you sure this is the right apartment and the right person?"

Officer Mack looked at me, pointed to the door, nodded his head and said "She's there".

I banged on the door again and said "Listen up, you have 3 seconds to open this door or it comes off the hinges".

The male voice was insisting "You have the wrong apartment, if you kick it in you will have an issue with me" Who was this guy kidding? What issue would that be?

Mike "I suggest you move away from the door or open it, one, two, three…"

My foot went straight through that cheap hollow core door, but now I could reach my hand through the hole and undo the lock. The apartment was no Four Seasons to begin with, but drug addicts have a way of messing up a place pretty quickly.

They had only been there for a day, and it was already looking like four crack heads had been sleeping on the floor and wiping their ass with the drapes.

I walked through the entry way into the living room and yelled "come out".

That is when I met up with what the owner of the male voice had called his "issue".

I heard the male voice say "get him" and a pit bull came rushing at me from the bed room.

Holy shit! My heart was about to popped out of my chest, I did not come all this way to get mauled by this dog, and I quickly pulled out my mace and blasted the dog straight in the face from 5 feet away.

The three officers had drawn their weapons at the same time I pulled out the mace, no one was taking any chances.

The pit bull whimpered from the blast of mace that caught him in the eyes and open mouth, he turned around and took a few steps back, then bent down and started rubbing his face in the carpet to try and wipe away the irritant from his eyes.

After only a few seconds, he got up and leaped at me from across the room, knocking me down and pinning my back to the floor with his paws on my chest.

Instead of tearing my face off, he started to lick me all the while whimpering, he was only a puppy.

I shouted at the officers "don't shoot, don't shoot, he's not dangerous" and to their credit the poor little guy didn't take a slug.

I rolled to my side, got Fido off of me and got to my feet.

I walked into the bedroom and started looking around, when I opened the closet Lisa was there and she did not put up a fight, I was able to cuff her with ease.

Just as I finished cuffing her, the mouth piece of resistance and commander of all canine forces popped up from under the bed. One look at this bum and you could tell he was a bad addict, 120lb skinny little fuck, with yellow teeth and matted hair.

He had an annoying voice, and he was cussing at me, telling me I had no right to do XY and Z.

He started getting a little too close for comfort, and one of the officers walked towards us to try and create space between hand cuffed Lisa, me and this idiot.

I guided Lisa towards Officer Courtney and turned to face this guy.

Mike "Back off buddy, I am hear for Lisa, consider yourself lucky I don't press charges against you for the pit bull attack"

He was getting in my face, trying to egg me on and at this point he was definitely under my skin.

He made one big mistake and that was to put hands on me, trying to grab my jacket just as I was about to leave the room.

I turned around, grabbed his left wrist and slapped a pair of cuffs

32

on it, then pulled it up, turned him around, forced him to the floor and cuffed both wrists together behind his back.

I asked the third officer to watch oh so mighty but now cuffed on the floor, Mr. Crack Head.

I stepped into the living room where Lisa was standing with Officer Courtney.

Mike "Lisa, who is this guy, is he your boyfriend?"

Lisa "Yes"

Mike "What's his name?"

Lisa "Jerry"

Mike "What's his last name?"

Lisa "Andrade, Jerry Andrade"

Lisa was a girl from a good family, she must have hooked up with this low life who got her into his lifestyle.

I turned to Officer Courtney and said "Officer Courtney, can I ask you for a favor?" Officer Courtney was enjoying every minute of the morning's action and he seemed eager to help, even more so than before.

Officer Courtney "Sure Mike, what can I do for you?"

Mike "Can you see if a one Jerry Andrade has an outstanding warrant in the greater Denver area by any chance?"

Officer Courtney Smiled at me Cheshire Grin style and said "I'll be back in 10 minutes" He was back in 5.

Officer Courtney "Mr. Quintana, Jerry has an outstanding warrant in Adams county for J walking"

Boy oh boy did I want to hear the words "outstanding warrant" in the context of one Jerry Andrade.

Did that little dumbass ever choose the wrong time to pop off to the wrong bounty hunter, and now I had a big old hard on for him. I walked into the bedroom, Jerry was still on the carpet facing the floor.

Mike "Guess what Jerry, you get to go on a romantic road trip with your girlfriend back to Adams County"

Jerry "You can't do that man, you've got no right to touch me, I'm going to sue your ass and all of your hillbilly backward asses for this shit, I'm going to…."

Mike "You're going to come back to Colorado with me, because I have this shinny little badge and you have an outstanding warrant for J walking"

Jerry "That's bullshit, you can't take me half way across the country on some shitty little J walking crap?"

Mike "Oh....Watch me"

Had that little stoner just kept him mouth shut, he would have been free to cook meth, get high, deal drugs or do any version of his American dream, but now he was mine, and the fun was just getting started.

I told Officer Courtney and Mack that I was going down to my vehicle and that I'd be back in a minute.

In the back of my car I carry a few extra pieces just in case, and now was just such a "just in case" moment.

I walked back up to the room with a paddle lock and two extra pieces of 4ft long chain.

One of the lengths of chain went around TweedleDee aka Lisa's waist and the other went around Tweedle Dumbass aka Jerry's waist. I then paddle locked the two together and transferred their cuffs from the back to the front.

I also put leg irons on Lisa, I didn't want her getting any ideas of running away.

Lisa turned to me with a concerned look on her face and said "what's going to happen to Puddles?" She was looking at the poor drooling Pit Bull, "can we call my neighbor in unit 207? Her name is Ellen, she loves Puddles, maybe she will agree to hold him until my mom can get him?"

Officer Courtney sent the third officer to fetch Ellen who was shocked at the hole in the door, the state of the apartment and the three officers now standing in it, but she agreed to take Puddles.

We walked down stairs to my vehicle, I told Jerry to get into the back of the car through the front passengers seat and sit in the back, while Lisa had no choice but to move with him and settle in the front seat, the chain connecting them was just long enough to settle between the two front seats.

If Jerry yanked the chain Lisa got pulled, if Lisa moved forward, Jerry got yanked forward.

Outside my car, I thanked officers Courtney and Mack as well as

34

the other three officers who accompanied me.

Mike "Thanks guys, you made this much easier than it could have been"

Officer Courtney "Much obliged to help and if you're ever back in these parts, be sure to make a social call there Mr. Quintana.

You going to be OK getting these two back like that all the way to Denver?"

Mike "Me? I'm going to be just fine, I don't know about those two, never transferred anyone like this before"

Officer Courtney "You got your hands full" Courtney smiled, I shook his hand and off we went.

We got back on the 64 going north heading towards Charleston. Once we got to Charleston, we headed west towards Lexington.

At first the two grumbled about the cuffs being too tight, and Jerry moaned about being uncomfortable, he couldn't find a good spot to relax without yanking Lisa.

I suggested they both just relax and remain still, for both of their sakes.

Outside of Lexington they needed to catch a toilet break.

I found a rest spot along the 64 and walked them to the bathroom connected at the waist. That chain wasn't coming off until we hit the Jail.

We walked into the men's bathroom, Lisa was frowning from the moment she got placed in cuffs but was more quite than Jerry, but now she looked horrified.

Lisa "Can you please undo this chain so that I can go, I have nowhere to run"

Mike "Nope"

Lisa "How am I supposed to pull down my clothes in chains being tied to Jerry"

Mike "I don't know, the two of you are geniuses, figure it out"
Jerry and Lisa walked into the stall, Jerry helped Lisa pull her bottom down, she sat on the can and he stood by, then it was Jerry's turn.

Love is a strange thing, it's great when everything is peaches and cream or a garden of roses, but when Jerry's junky ass went off Lisa was not too impressed with his "Garden of Roses".

Lisa "God Damn Jerry"

Jerry "What?"

Lisa "You are disgusting, you know that?" I couldn't help it and just full on laughed out load. She was discovering that love isn't just blind, but it deaf, dumb, has no sense of taste and is borderline retarded. At least Jerry was restoring her sense of smell.

The two were turning from a pair of love birds into two cats in a bag. They got each other ready grumbling and snapping at each other the whole time.

We left the rest area and once we were past Lexington, Dumbass decided that being uncomfortable and potty humiliated wasn't enough, he wanted to start belly aching again and playing games.

Jerry "Mike, I need to take a shit"

Mike "you just did"

Jerry "If you don't stop I will take a shit in my pants, in your car and you'll have to clean me, buy me new clothes or smell dukie all the way to Colorado, do you want that?"

Mike "If you do that I will call the local fire department and they will strip you on the side of the highway and hose you down, now stop fucking around".

Jerry was none too bright, but he was starting to get it, I wasn't playing around, the more he fucked around, the more I didn't care and the less comfortable they were going to be.

At around 9pm I decided to hit a diner just past St. Louis, and then find a motel.

I spotted a little mom and pop place off of the freeway and turned in to the parking lot.

When you are misbehaving and there is no one there to see you do it, that's one thing, but when you're being shamed publicly it is a little more difficult to act as if you just don't care.

I marched the pair into the diner, found a booth and sat down.

There were about 25 people in the diner when we entered, including children and a few old folks, but not an eye was looking at anything else but me and my two fugitives.

There was a family of four, a young couple with a 7 year old boy and a 3 year old girl in one of the booths.

The little boy turned to his dad and said "daddy, why are they in

36

chains, did they do something bad?"

Lisa and Jerry's heads just turned to look down at the floor.

We sat down and ordered, I was responsible for feeding them, but I wasn't responsible for putting the food in their mouths.

In spite of all the hardships of eating with cuffed hands, the two polished off everything that was placed in front of them.

We then pulled up to a Motel 6, I parked the car outside of the office.

Mike "You two stay right here, don't try anything, the car is child proofed anyway"

In the office I told the receptionist that we needed a room with two beds, I also told them that I was a bounty hunter with two fugitives and that we will be sleeping together in the same room.

Once in the room, I made sure Lisa and Jerry went for another bathroom trip which culminated in another argument.

I then cuffed them to the bed with some extra chain and tried to get some sleep.

It wasn't the greatest night's sleep, but I woke up at 7am ready to make the rest of the way back to Colorado.

The two were finally behaving, Jerry had been quite all morning.

Lisa asked if she and Jerry could smoke a cigarette, and I agreed to let them sit quietly on the bench outside the Motel 6 room, while I was in the car, and let them have some alone time.

Once back in the car we made good time and by Friday night we were back in Denver.

I pulled up to the Adams county Jail and got the couple out of the car.

The travel was such a physical ordeal, that the two almost seemed happy to be getting locked up.

We walked up to the reception area and were greeted once again by Officer Sanchez.

Officer Sanchez "What do we have here Quintana?"

Mike "Lisa Bishop, here's her paper work, and this is Jerry Andrade. If you look him up, you'll find he's got an outstanding warrant for J walking"

Officer Sanchez "Why do you have them paddle locked together?"

37

Mike "Had to transport them from West Virginia together"
Officer Sanchez "You went all the way to West Virginia?"

Mike "Yes Sir"

Officer Sanchez "I can see a decent bounty for Bishop, but you picked up and carried Andrade all the way to Colorado for a J walking warrant?"

Mike "He pissed me off"

Officer Sanchez "So you arrested Andrade and drove him across the country, just because he pissed you off?"

Mike "Yes sir"

Officer Sanchez "Remind me never to piss you off, OK? Officer Sanchez was laughing at his own joke.

Mike "Yes Sir" I left the Jail, called Jason, told him I have Lisa in Adams county jail, and then called you Amit, can you believe this bounty?

Me "Mike, you've always told me the truth, but I tell you what?"
Mike "What?"

Me "Remind me never to piss you off either"

Mike erupted once again into his contagious laugh, and once again I couldn't help but join him.

8. TOP OF THE LIST

Mike "At any given time I have a case load of about 20 files. Some of them I can finish within a day, others take more than a month, but they all get worked in some way, shape or form"

"If a tip comes in and that window of opportunity pops up for me to catch a fugitive, I will drop everything in order to make it through that window.

From time to time a bondsman will tell me he needs a file closed ASAP and I will put that case on the top of my list. But rest assured I will start developing leads on all my cases within hours of picking them up.

Now there's a special place in my heart, and oh boy is it a special place, for any sex offender's file that enters my case load.

Predators will get top priority and I will start driving these cases harder, the more of a predator you are, the harder I will try to catch you and the size of the bond doesn't even matter.

I could be working a $50,000 bond, but your measly $2500 will cross my path, so guess what "Mr. Oral copulation with a minor?" today's your lucky day, you made it to the top of my list.

Making it to the top of the list is one thing, but making it to the top of the list whilst I sport a big old hard on for you while I chase you down, now that's a real special kind of fugitive.

And to get to that super special fugitive status, you not only have to throw the sex offender 7 to get in to the game, but now you have to taunt me and hey presto bingo asshole, you are not only at the top of the list but your file is on fire.

A quick word about the bounty hunting profession, just because Hollywood likes to throw a bounty hunter into a movie from time to time and now the bounty hunter profession sounds "cool" or maybe you think that its easy money scooping up fugitives, does not mean that anyone can do this job.

You may fancy yourself as a "Bounty Hunter" in order to gain the respect of your peers or it may be a cool thing to tell a chick in a bar, but this is a job you have to love doing.

I get called in to fix cases that got burned by wanna be bounty hunters, who finished watching Boba Fett in a Star Wars movie on

39

Monday, got their certification on Tuesday, picked up their first bounty on Wednesday, fucked it up by Thursday and are back to selling insurance policies by Friday.

I get a call from a bondsman in the Denver area, asking me to come down to his office, he needed help fixing a case that got burned by a rookie.

When I picked up the file it seemed a little strange, it was a $2500 no hold bond for a sexual assault on a minor, which is a very low amount for such an offense.

The story was that 28 year old Dominic "Dickey" Martin was having a problem growing up.

He and his buddies still liked to hang out at the old high school haunts and try to pick up girls.

Dickey probably had a low self-esteem issue and found it easier to hit on teens and young twenty year olds, which he took a step too far when he roofied a 16 year old at a bar.

The girl woke up in his bed, freaked out and got mom to press charges.

The case went to trial and the judge let Dickey out on bail. Instead of manning up and showing up for sentencing, Dickey decided he could avoid the inevitable jail time and just ran.

 Getting a hunt back on track takes a bit of doing and I needed to check out all the addresses from the file, scope them out and get a feel for Dickey's whereabouts.

I wanted to check these places out, but I didn't want my presence being detected and further forcing Dickey into hiding.

In many ways I wanted him to get a sense that no one was looking for him, and maybe he would start popping up which would get me right back on his trail.

I kept things low key like this for about a week. One of the leads that popped up was a family member of Dickey's who owned a restaurant that me and Sonya like to frequent.

When I picked up the file I didn't know that there was any relationship between him and Dickey.

Sonya and I went there for dinner and had a chat with the owner. He told us he was related to Dickey but he hadn't seen him in a while. Dickey had been getting into all kinds of trouble, small stuff but he wasn't getting his life together and the owner tried to distance himself from Dickey.

Even though he didn't know where he was, he pointed us in the direction of Dickeys grandparents, who lived in Lakewood.

He told us that there were quite a few relatives living in that same complex of townhouses. His sister lived across the street with her family, an uncle lived two houses down from the grandparents and there were more Martins on neighboring streets.

Once again, this slowed the tracking process down, there were entirely too many potential eyeballs in the neighborhood keeping a watchful eye.

I decided to check out the neighborhood anyway, just go out, and find a spot to park within binocular distance of the grandparent's house.

If me and Sonya can spend a peaceful night at home together in front of the TV, we can spend an afternoon in the car with a few snacks and a pair of binoculars scoping out a neighborhood, easy. So we observed the house, different family members came and went, but no sign of Dickey.

At one point a younger man walked in with what appeared to be his girlfriend, but they never left. It was getting dark and it started to snow, so we decided to call it a day.

We returned in the morning and got right back to business.
At around 9am the grandmother stepped outside, got in her car and started to back out of the driveway.

We decided to follow her and pulled out slowly, passing the house and keeping our distance.

Grandma Martin made a few shopping stops, nothing special and returned home.

Just as we were pulling up, a Jeep drove up and parked on the side of the street.

A man in his twenties stepped out and followed Grandma Martin into the house. Sonya turned to me and said it wasn't Dickey, it looked to her like the guy that came in with his girlfriend the day before.

I didn't want to waste any more time on this location so I decided to burn it, meaning let Dickey know that we are watching this location and force him to move to another hideout.

I walked up to the porch where Grandpa Martin was now sitting and reading a paper.

Mike "Good Morning Mr. Martin"

Grandpa "Good Morning" I pulled out the badge hanging from the chain around my neck.

Mike "I am looking for Dickey, has he been here in the last week"

Grandpa "No, I haven't seen him" he turned and called for his wife who appeared on the porch.

Facing the Grandmother I repeated the question.

Grandma "No, I haven't seen him"

Mike "In that case you won't mind if I take a quick look inside and see for myself, do you?"

Grandma "Go ahead, if you have to"

I walked through the front door and the entry way, past the kitchen and the first bedroom, they were empty.

One of the bedroom doors a few feet ahead of me closed from the inside and I walked up to it, attempting to turn the knob but it was now locked. I banged on the door.

Mike "open up" A female voice on the inside replied "one minute" and I could hear some shuffling going on behind the door.

If Dickey was inside, I didn't want him jumping out of a window so I forced the issue.

Mike "Open the door right now or I'll kick it down"

Grandma Martin was standing behind me, she got a little panicked and said "That's his brother Kenny, Dickey's not hear, I promise" The door opened and I let myself in, it was indeed his brother and the girlfriend from yesterday, but no Dickey.

Mike "When was the last time you saw your brother?" Kenny was looking at the floor nervously, I knew he was about to lie to me.

Kenny "I haven't seen him in over a month".

Mike "When you do, let him know I am looking for him"

I left my card with the Grand Parents, letting them know that if they should see him it would be in their grandson's best interests to give me a call.

Now the place was burnt good and proper, Dickey would not be spending any time there for sure.

I had to go to the court that afternoon on another case, but while I was there I decided to look up Dickey's bond.

It appeared that he had a girlfriend by the name of Shaleena who cosign for him on a previous bond, I pulled the number and was about to give her a call when my phone rang.

Mike "Hello"

Dickey "This is Dickey"

Mike "Oh good, listen Dominic, you need to come in, I will meet you at your grandparent's house today…" Dickey started to talk over me and cut me off.

Dickey "Listen asshole, I'm not coming in"

Mike "it's better that you do, this thing ain't gonna go away"

Dickey started to laugh as if the joke was on me.

Mike "Listen, come in and you can spare yourself, your family and friends a lot of trouble".

Dickey "Now you listen asshole, I'm too smart, too slick, too fast and I am having too much fun to come on in, you ain't never going to catch me. That other dipshit who was chasing me couldn't catch me and neither can you" He trailed off with an annoying laugh.

Mike "I'm going to catch you, you hear me, I'm going to catch you and there's no way I am not going to catch you, you little punk"

If his intention was to get under my skin, mission accomplished.

Dickey "In that case come look for me in Vegas, I'll be at the Wynn with 2 hookers and a bottle of grey goose, ha ha ha…"

Mike "If you hang out on the Eifel Tower I will pop up behind you and catch you, If you go to the Great Wall of China I will find you and catch you, if you hide behind a buffalo in Yellowstone park I will wear a wolf skin crawl through the brush and catch you, there is nowhere for you to hide slick, I will catch you!"

Dickey was laughing really hard now, peppering his chuckles with little hoots and "Really".

Dickey "See you in Vegas asshole" he hung up.

What did I say earlier about getting to the top of the list? Dickey in one conversation just did it all and now I was going to get him even if I lost money on this one.

There is something that happens to me when I get mad, once I get there and I have blown off some steam, I then start enjoying every bit of the catch. It is almost like a Cheetah who can taste it's pray as it is chasing it seconds before the catch itself. And now I could already see the stupid look on Dickey's face when I finally had him face down and in cuffs.

As soon as I got off the phone with Dickey, I dialed Shaleena's number, the phone rang.

Shaleena "Hello"

Mike "Hi Shaleena, this is Mike Quintana, I am looking for your boyfriend Dominic"

Shaleena "We are not together anymore, who gave you my number?"

Mike "You were the Consignor on his last bond, I got your number off the paperwork"

Shaleena "Like I said, I no longer see him" She sounded sweet.

Mike "I need to find Dominic, he's in trouble. Can we meet tomorrow?"

Shaleena "Sure, anything to help"

Mike "Starbucks tomorrow at 10am OK?"

Shaleena agreed to help, this was a big step in the right direction.

I decided to leave everything until tomorrow and went about following another case.

My phone rang at 1am, it was an unidentified number.

Mike "Hello" There was no response, just a bunch of people talking in the background, so I hung up.

The phone rang again like this about 3 more times, and on the third time it was the familiar voice of Dickey.

Dickey "Ha,Ha,Ha you're never going to catch me… Ha,Ha,Ha…" he hung up. Dickey was enjoying himself but not for long.

I got a call from Shaleena the following day, she needed to postpone our meeting, pushing things back another day and then a week.

While I was waiting to meet up with Shaleen, I would get calls from Dickey, sometimes at 1am other times in the middle of the day but he was always laughing and enjoying his final numbered days of freedom.

Mike "Hello"

Dickey "Ha,Ha,Ha… I wanted to invite you to a pool party I am having in Los Angeles Ha,Ha,Ha…"

Mike "Oh ya?"

Dickey "Ya, Bring your Speedo, Ha,Ha,Ha… I told you, I'm too slick and you're too slow Ha,Ha,Ha…

Mike "Keep laughing it up funny boy, I'll be seeing you very soon"

Dickey "I'm Too Slick and you're too slow". This time I hung up on him.

I was getting the feeling that Shaleena was dragging her feet because she still had some feeling for Dickey, I decided to call her and apply some pressure.

Mike "Hi Shaleena, its Mike"

Shaleena "Oh…Hello Mike…I was going to…" She sounded a little nervous.

Mike "Call Me? Listen Shaleena, We need to meet, Dickey is in a lot of trouble, if he doesn't come in things will get worse and you may be the one to help him. If you care about him you will do everything to help him, you do want to help him don't you?"

I said the last words with authority and a mix of care.

Shaleena "Yes, I want to help"

Mike "Can you meet me today?"

Shaleena "OK" We agreed to go back to the original meeting place, Starbucks in Westminster at 1pm and she showed up on time.

Shaleena was in her 20's, 5ft 5" with straight black hair, she was cute, sweet and my previous hunches of caring for Dickey even though they weren't together anymore were all true.

She offered to take me to a friend's house in Denver where Dickey and his buddies would hang out.

I drove my vehicle and she accompanied me in the front passenger's seat to show the way.

When we pulled up to the street, I parked half a block away from the house.

I could see through the binoculars a group of guys standing in the front yard.

I counted 6 individuals and there was Dickey, with a beer in his hand, laughing and having a good old time.

45

Attempting to arrest him in the presence of his buddies may not have been the healthiest thing for me, 7 against 1 were not the type of odds I liked at all. I decided to try to use Shaleena's help.

Mike "Do you think you can get Dickey to come to you?"

Shaleena "I can try"

Mike "He knows where you live right?"

Shaleena "Yes"

Mike "Set up a meeting with him at your place"

Shaleena picked up her cell phone and dialed Dickeys number, all the while I was watching him laugh it up with his buddies in the front yard.

Shaleena "Hi Dickey, its Shaleena"

While she was talking to him, I pulled out and started driving down the street towards the house. That familiar Cheetah feeling was kicking in big time.

I was thinking about how I was going to catch this punk or maybe you could call it daydreaming, but I took a left exiting the street to an adjacent part of the neighborhood within sight of the front yard, it was a bit too close for comfort, did he see us?

Shaleena "Do you miss me? What was that, I can't hear you?" Something got Dickeys attention, I hoped he didn't spot us turning down the side street.

If Dickey got spooked by my vehicle or saw something, he didn't say anything to Shaleena, who was able to set up the "Rendezvous".

Mike "Remember, I will be on the street in my vehicle watching his every move, all you have to do is leave your front door open, OK?"

Shaleena "OK, But what if he saw us? She seemed worried.

Mike "Let's hope he didn't. I'll call you in the morning before I head out".

I was salivating now, it was like I went to the Hunting department at Big Five, got me a bear trap, put it in the woods and all I had to do was come back tomorrow and bag me a moose.

That cocky little prick had no idea how short lived his life on the run was about to become.

At 11pm my phone rang, it was an unidentified number, but I had a pretty good idea who was on the other line.

Mike "Hello" I was trying to hide my confidence and conjure up
that old indignant anger I had when Dickey first tried to egg me on.

Dickey "Ha,Ha,Ha…listen, listen…." He turned his phone
towards the sound of a room full of people talking, it sounded like a
bar.

"I'm in LA hommie, we missed you at the pool party, everyone
wanted to get a glimpse of you in your Speedo, Ha,Ha,Ha…." He
sounded really pleased with himself.

Mike "Listen to me you little punk, I'm going to get you, keep
laughing" I wasn't that mad, but I couldn't give him any hints that
he was being set up.

Dickey "I know, I know, you're going to get me, and I'm a little
punk, but I tell you what, I'm having a blast at the Skybar here in
Hollywood man.

You've got to come down here, there's this 6ft 4 bouncer called
Bernardo, he's from Italy, really gay but he sounds like your type.
In fact I told him all about you, he's dying to meet you, and now
that they've changed the laws in California you two would make a
great couple.

Think about it, he could bounce you could bounty, then you two
could cuddle together in bed and tell each other you love each other
in a deep voice, Ha,Ha,Ha….really sweet don't you think?"

Maybe he was just trying to get my goat, or maybe he had seen
me turn down the side street earlier that day and was just trying to
get some extra information out of me, but I couldn't let a thing slip.
Mike "When I catch you, you'll be someone's jail bitch I promise
you"

Dickey "Listen, if you change your mind, I'll introduce you to
Bernardo, anyway got to go, bye…Ha,Ha,Ha…" and he hung up.
Tomorrow couldn't have come fast enough and I woke up ready for
the day.

At 11am I called Shaleena, reminded her to leave her door open
and headed over to Westminster.

I parked on the street 200ft from the entrance to her apartment
complex.

5pm rolled around and like clockwork, Dickey dressed in a red
Jacket and a baseball cap popped out of the adjacent side street and

47

walked right through the entrance.

I waited for about a minute before exiting my car and entered the complex behind him.

I walked towards Shaleena's first floor apartment, looking from side to side making sure I hadn't been seen.

I walked up to Shaleena's apartment, I could hear voices from behind the door.

I turned the knob slowly, it was unlocked, and I pushed the door open.

Shaleena was standing in the living room facing the door, and in front of her with his back to the door was Dickey.

My adrenaline was pumping and that Cheetah saliva was now flooding my mouth, I pulled my Taser from its holster, pointed it at Dickeys back and said "ON YOUR KNEES!!!"

Dickey gave a startled glance backwards over his shoulder, turned a shade of red and got to his knees immediately"

Dickey "You bitch, you fucking bitch, I can't believe you did this to me!" He was shouting at Shaleena who looked hurt, her only response was to fold her arms and take a deep breath.

Mike "Shut up and put your arms above your head" Dickey raised his arms, I walked up behind him and with the heel of my shoe pushed him over. He landed on his belly with a thud.

I was about to holster the Taser when Dickey did a barrel roll to the right, I squeezed the trigger to the Taser and the barbs shot out of the end lodging into his back right through his jacket.

I squeezed the trigger and 50,000 volts went right through his little punk ass body, causing him to spaz and yell at the same time.

Mike "If you move I will hit you with the juice again, now put your hands behind your back, do it now!"

Dickey placed his hands behind his back and I cuffed him.

I walked him to the car and got him in to the front passenger seat. We were heading for Jefferson County Jail.

Dickey was mouthy and talking all kinds of shit, but I didn't care, he was in my possession.

Dickey "It was you who drove by the house yesterday wasn't it"

Mike "Yup that was me Dominic"

Dickey "Oh, you were too big of a pussy to come and get me

when I was hanging with my friends, weren't you?"

Mike "That's exactly right, but look at you now, your shit all fucked up and in chains. You are going to meet the Judge in a few days who will have you in the slammer for about 4 years for that assault on a minor, remember?"

Dickey "I didn't do it!"

Mike "Of course you didn't, people get locked up for roofying minors for no reason every day"

Dickey "Fuck you"

We drove in silence for a minute or so, and then Dickey start to cry, which caught me off guard.

Mike "Really? You were all Johnny tough guy for the last 4 weeks egging me on and now you're gonna cry?"

Dickey "I can't go to prison man"

Mike "Face it you're going to prison, you don't pass go, and you don't collect $400".

We pulled up to the Jefferson county Jail, Dickey was really dragging his feet getting up the driveway towards the door.

The drive was a short drive, when I initially placed Dickey in cuffs I didn't think he was going to try any funny stuff because he was so compliant, so I didn't put ankle Irons on him.

All of a sudden Mr. Molasses feet decided to make a mad dash to freedom. He wasn't 4 feet away when I grabbed his cuffs from behind and yanked them up towards the back of his head causing him pain and stopping him dead in his tracks.

Mike "Where do you think you're going?"

Dickey "I am not going to prison man, I am telling you"

I gave Dickey a hard shove, and we entered the waiting room where Dickey finally found himself in a cell where he belonged.

On the way home a familiar feeling of satisfaction went through my body, it is as good as any drug or sex.

It is a feeling of being of service in the hands of justice, and if you've never experienced anything like this I can tell you it makes everything worthwhile.

9. MOLESTERS CAN'T BOX

Mike "I love boxing, I've been involved with boxing, boxers and fighters my whole life, and I will probably be in it until the day I die, unless there is a good boxing club in the next life as well. I got it from my pops and it's definitely in my genes"

There is something that happens to you when you decide to engage in combat and train for it.

It isn't only your body that toughens up and becomes athletic, fit and capable of being pushed to the limit or enduring pain, it is your character that will toughen up as well, they will go hand in hand.

The best thing a young man can develop in today's world is mental toughness, to cope with it.

With that comes an understanding of not just strength in yourself, but the weakness of others.

I can't say I've ever had this conversation with boxers, but those guys that have trained or are involved with training a fighter, somehow naturally understand strength and weakness in the world around them.

You've heard the saying "I'm not a fighter, I'm a lover" that saying is the biggest piece of bullshit ever concocted by a weak guy looking to get out of a fight. I'd say fighters are lovers, period, end of story.

When you train hard, get punched and dish a few punches out yourself, there is nothing better than being loved, it is the best medicine a fighter can have, and whenever you see a HBO 24/7 doc about an upcoming Vegas fight, you will always see the fighter with his family and kids

I'd go as far as saying that a man that has not toughened up and felt the resistance of another person's will, may seek dominance over someone or something that they perceive to be more vulnerable than them, and when this really goes south, they will pray on innocence.

Case in point was this child molester I busted a few years ago. One of the bondsman I work with calls me for a $15,000 no holds bond for a child molester from Aurora Co. by the name of James L. Southridge.

The file had his picture, a non-descript white guy, 5ft 5, brown eyes, light brown hair, if you saw him in the street "Child Molester" or "Pedophile" would not be the first thing that would cross your mind.

In fact, you would probably have passed him by and not thought anything at all, and maybe that is how animals like James simply go under the radar.

The cosigner was his girlfriend at the time, Samantha Cole, a 32 year old Afro American Girl, I had her telephone number and address in Aurora.

It was the beginning of winter and the nights were getting darker earlier.

I didn't want to go looking for this guy in the dark, so I headed over to the girlfriend's house at 9am to snoop around and see if maybe I could pick Jimmy boy up bright and early.

Nothing like starting your day off with a check mark on your to do list that could potentially free up your whole day, and the promise of a good payday at the end of the week, right?

I pulled up to the house, it was a two bedroom house with what looked like a single room addition in the back.

The house was located in a nice working class neighborhood.

I snooped around, it was quite, no motion in or around the place as far as I could see (there goes my check mark), so I decided to return in the evening.

Another reason I didn't really want to go looking for him in the dark but would do it if I had to, is because from experience the local Sheriff's department did not always come out to assist bounty hunters, only in cases of known firearms potentially being involved.

When entering a house it is always prudent to call the local Sheriff's department, especially when it involves harder crimes that carry stiffer sentences such as drugs or pedophilia, the fugitives know what they are facing and are more likely to be less cooperative than a driver's license revocation case.

So I came back at around 8pm and just parked my car on the street and waited.

A big part of Bounty Hunting is waiting a fugitive out, we are creatures of habit, and we will not stay indoors hiding forever.

Sooner or later a fugitive will pop their head out, which is all the cause I need in order to arrest them.

At around 9pm I saw two men walking down the street, they approach the house, one of them fit dear James's profile.

They walked up to the house, the door opened and in they went. Once the door was closed I walked up to the house, pulled my badge out so that it hung from around my neck, and knocked on the door. Samantha opened it.

Mike "Where's James Sam?"

Samantha "I don't know, I haven't see him in over a week"

Mike "Bullshit, Don't lie to me, I saw him walk in 2 minutes ago"

I side stepped her into the house and started looking around. To my surprise, in the living room which was right adjacent to the entrance, were Samantha's 3 daughters in front of the TV, her 9 year old, a 14 year old and her 9 month baby daughter.

I walked towards the two rooms, looked quickly in both and then the kitchen but there was no sign of James or his buddy.

Samantha was walking behind me repeating the same thing over and over "He's not here, I told you etc…"

Next to the kitchen was a door, I figured it was probably the door to the add on room I saw earlier in the day from the outside.

I went to open it and Samantha said with some indignation "hey, that's private"

Bullshit, ain't nothing private when you cosign for a Molester and I'm on his case.

I turned the nob but it was locked, the door was not your cheap HomeDepot hollow core door either, I could hear noises behind the door which was locked from the inside.

The situation I walked in on was worse than I could ever have imagined.

An irresponsible single mother of 3 girls, cosigning for a convicted sex offender who has skipped bail, and is not registered with the local authorities, could this get worse?

I wasn't waiting for anyone to open that door, and with one kick busted the jam and that's when I saw what worse looked like.

On several computer monitors playing at the same time were images of child porn, this was Jimmies porn shack, filled with the depravity of a broken human mind devoid of a moral compass.

It isn't only misery that loves company, but apparently Pedophile birds of a feather will flock together and share sick and twisted files, hence Jimmies buddy who was now white as a ghost with his back up against one of the desks.

I almost lost it, I was about to go Judge Dredd on James and sidekick when I took a breath and composed myself.

My hands were shaking with rage, all I could say under my breath was "get over here".

James who two seconds ago had popped out of his computer chair, walked towards me then passed through the doorway and into the kitchen, leaving his friend frozen behind him, I followed.

I was about to pulled my cuffs out of my right jacket pocket when James turned around in the center of the kitchen, and took a swing at me, a right hook right at my head, which was slow, clumsy and weak.

The years of boxing kicked in, and in less than a fraction of a second I did a little back bend, moving my head out of the way of James fist and countered him with an over the top right which landed right on the chin and put James on his ass.

James was rocked pretty good, had this been a Vegas fight the ref would have waved it off because Jimmy wasn't making the count. I pounced, rolled him over, cuffed the right hand, then the left behind his back.

As James was coming to, Samantha was just standing there with a shocked look on her face, that's when I lost it.

Mike "Are you out of your mind? If you don't care about yourself, good, you shouldn't, you are a piece of shit just like this piece of shit I have cuffed on your floor.

But to expose your 3 daughters is insane, you are a shitty mother, you deserve to have your kids taken away"

Samantha burst into tears, I pulled James's handcuffs from behind, got him up off the floor and left.

Thinking back, Samantha was in on James's Child porn racket, it probably paid a few bills and she conveniently turned a blind eye to the immorality of it all.

I guess his sidekick buddy was there purchasing his dose of sickness from James, it was a mutually beneficial relationship and no one was going to tell on anyone.

Once at my vehicle, I sat James in the front passenger's seat and took off towards Arapahoe County Jail.

We drove in silence, I was thinking about everything that just happened and a bunch of "what ifs" started to crop into my mind. What if James had a father like mine, would he have turned out to be the little sick piece of shit that he is today?

Or when James was torturing little insects as a 7 year old, what if his father had taken him to a martial arts class or a boxing Gym, do you think he would have still turned out to be a predator?

No way! If someone had given this guy some boxing classes, he wouldn't have been getting his jollies off on child porn, been convicted of molestation or joined the denizens of the Magen computer.

In the very least he would have been able to cold cock me in the kitchen with a good enough right hook, but had he been able to do that I wouldn't have been in his girlfriend's kitchen in the first place, it's all a little bit like the Twilight Zone, isn't it?

I had my thoughts and my theories, but I needed some input from James, what was going through his mind?

Mike "What possessed you to get into this Child Porn James? What were you thinking?"

James just stared ahead and broke a big smile, which got under my skin, my water had just been boiling and he was turning up the flame again.

Mike "Don't smile, this is nothing to smile about"

James turned to me with an even bigger smile on his face and said "You should consider yourself lucky I wasn't looking at your daughter"

I took my right hand off the wheel and bitch slapped James with the back of my hand.

You wanna swing at me, that's mano a mano stuff which I'm OK with, you start talking mad shit about my family? Boy, you must really be looking for trouble.

We drove the rest of the way in silence.

I didn't know the officer that accepted James L. Southridge at the Jail, he just took one look at the paper work and said "James, James,

James… we've been waiting for you, there's a cell with your name on it, nice and comfy, all warmed up for you"

He turned to me and said "we've been waiting for this one now for a while, good Job Quintana"

James sounded a little urgent when he turned to the officer "I want to be placed in Protective custody"

Officer, "Sorry James, you are going into general pop"
It was 12:05 in the morning, my papers were signed, I was tired and it was time to go home.

10. THE SIZE OF THE DOG AND HIS BACON

It's only 8:30pm on a Thursday when my phone goes off, It's Mike. This is a normal hour for him to be calling, which means that it must be some boxing related news, right?

Me "Hey Mike, what's up?"

Mike "You'll never believe it, I just caught the biggest blackest guy you have ever see" (Let me take this opportunity to assure you that Mike isn't racist, he just paints a visual with the necessary tools, really quick)

I got the file 2 days ago, no picture no nothing, just an address and a description.

It just said, Julius Joans III wanted for Identity theft and his address was in Aurora (a suburb of Denver).

The bond was for $2500 and it was a no bond hold meaning, a judge deemed Mr. Julius to be too much of a risk to society, therefore once he's caught, he is not getting released, period.

Why? Because Mr. Julius had no problem slipping back into society once he made bail, stealing another identity and repeating his hustle all over again, this judge was no one's fool.

So I drive to his house, a complex of single story suburban homes with a wooden fence around the property and a garage entry way.

Nothing special, except for the fact that Julius's car was up on a jack with a tire missing.

The gate to the house was facing the car about 4ft away, so even if he made a run for it, he ain't going nowhere, not without hoofing it. I like that feeling, anything that seems like a level playing field or mano a mano is fine with me, in fact I prefer it that way.

If I have to chase you by car, it's dangerous to the public, things can get out of control, and the bottom line is if that happens, I didn't do my job right.

Bounty hunting is not about being John Wayne or Starsky & Hutch and kicking down doors or flashing a dirty Harry 45 in a crack heads face.

It's about stealth, waiting for the right moment when the fugitive is not ready and catching him quick, with the least amount of bull shit, which as you'll see in dear Mr. Julius's case doesn't always happen.

Now as I said before, I didn't have a picture only a description, but the same is true for Julius, he doesn't know who I am either which gives me the advantage.

I parked my vehicle in a neighbor's parkway and made it around the back of Jules property, just as I am walking through the alley adjacent to the house, he appears.

Only in rare occasions do my instincts fail me, I knew Mr. Jones from the description instantly, bounty hunting will do that to you, it will sharpen your skills in areas that you will need for the job such as instant identification.

It wasn't the wildest stretch of the imagination either, how many 6ft 3", 28 year old 250lb brothers with a muscular physique are going to be roaming the same neighborhood suburb?

My reaction time had to be quick, so I pulled out my badge and told Julius he was under arrest, he said "who the fuck are you?"

And before I could tell him what's what, he took off around the property wall and entered into the town home from the back door.

I followed through the yard shooting for the front door. He probably had to navigate a couple of power rangers, an X Box, the kitchen, a love seat and open the door, so I beat him to the front porch, but he darted out the front and for some reason instead of heading down the street and the hell away from me he hung a right.

This appeared to lead back around the property to the same alley where we started, so I ran to the alley and sure enough a much panicked and winded Julius came right at me but this time the dumb and dumber routine was over.

I tackled him head on, put him on his back and placed my trusty Taser in his throat and shouted "if you give me any more shit I will mother fucking taze you in the goddamn throat, now roll over" it took him a minute or two but he finally complied.

Most people can't handle a person that much bigger than them, I am only 5ft 6', I could probably afford to lose 40lb which doesn't always help when you have to chase someone, but it sure comes in handy when you have to tackle a mother fucker.

This became even more apparent when I helped Jules up, a 250lb man is a lot of weight, I was just happy I didn't need to drag him to my car, which has been known to happen with a non-compliant fugitive from time to time.

Once in the car I asked him to extend his legs and placed ankle shackles on him.

He asked that I go back to the house and ask his wife for his wallet, which sounded reasonable enough.

So I rang the doorbell and out came Mrs. Jones, holly shit!!! Every pot has its lid but I am not sure who was supposed to be the pot and who was the lid in this equation.

Mr. Jones stood about 5ft 7' high and was probably of the same width, she was a whole lot of woman, approximately 220lb and now she was pissed.

She started with the usual profanity, about how I look, the nature of my horrible job, what nasty man I was (trust me, I am cleaning this up) and of course my penis size.

She followed me to the gate and once we were in front of the gate, she threw the wallet on the other side, up and over, so that it landed between the gate and the Jacked up car.

I moved towards the gate, once I opened it and I was just about to leave when she smashed it shut up against my ribs, which dropped me to the floor and up against the jacked car.

I stood up quick, wallet in hand, but big mama Jones wasn't done. She followed me to the car and continued to mouth off.

Julius saw all of this, and I told him I was going to call the Cops and file assault charges against his wife, which he begged me not to do, all the while yelling at the misses to go back into the house and chill.

I figured we had enough drama for one bounty and took off towards the Jail house, to deposit Julius, get my papers stamped and move on to the next bounty of the day.

You'd think that would be the end of it, but now it was Julius's turn. It really is beyond me, but I will never understand why a shackled fugitive on their way to the fun house finds the need to try and negotiate.

And their methods of negotiation are even nuttier than the reason why. Threats won't work, I already have you.

Swearing and cussing do not open car doors or loosen hand cuffs. Spitting will only get your shirt pulled over your head for the duration of the ride.

Now you can try to sweet talk me but let me ask you the reader, how many times do you think that has happened and how many times has it actually worked?

So Julius ran at the mouth all the way to the prison, what's new.

To be honest, I don't even remember what he said, what his insults were, his poor attempt at talking shit about my mama, what offer or bribe he made, who his thug friends with gangster connections were, how much pain those "friends" of his were going to inflict on me once they found out about how I miss treated him and blah blah blah... same old bullshit, just coming from another asshole.

I was expecting Officer Clark and Officer Sanchez to greet me as they usually do, with smiles on their faces and small talk, but this time it was more like shock and surprise.

Officer Sanchez who stands a mere 5'6 was looking around "what? You came alone? Where is the rest of your posse?

Mike "Posse? Nope, just me"

Officer Clark with a smile mixed with surprise lifted his eyes, shook his head and just said "I don't even want to know how you managed to nab this guy or how you shoe horned him into your car" They stamped my papers and off I went.

For the next few days following the arrest I had a hard time breathing, every time I took a breath I felt pain in my chest and back.

A visit to the doctor confirmed that I sustained a cracked rib due to the hit I took from Mrs. Jones.

I know what you're thinking, all of this for 10% of $2500?

A cracked rib for 250 bucks?

Bounties ad up quick, I can pull down an easy grand in a short few hours and on the rare occasion a cracked rib for what may appear to be peanuts.

The point is you never know if a job is going to be easy or not, and neither do I care, when it comes to my bacon or putting food on the table, my family comes first and you better believe my family is going to eat.

I have a job to do, it is not a job most people care to do, and for

59

some it may seem too hard or risky and yes, at times it is.
If you want a cushy job, don't bounty hunt, I never think about my comfort, only about the end result.

In this case it was more important for me to catch Julius and get paid, than it was for Julius to run and fight to be free, size didn't matter.

It is not the size of the dog in the fight, or the fight in the dog that matters, it is the importance of the bacon he is fighting for.

11. PINCHI COUSIN CHRIS

Mike "When I was 18, the family moved from Riverside CA. to Denver CO.

I love California but my heart is in the Rockies, mile high, clean air, cold winters and fresh air. You just can't beat it.

I have a lot of family in Colorado, and a bunch of them live here. I remember meeting my Cousin Chris, we are related from my mom's side of the family.

When I got here, we hung out and it was all good back in the day. I went my way and Chris went his, oh boy did he ever.

Chris got into a bunch of shit, drugs, slapping a girlfriend around etc... Not great behavior, but those were his choices.

In July 2011, I went on vacation with the misses to Cali.

I told my bondsman that I am off for a couple of weeks and they should not call me until I get back, because I won't drop my vacation to go chase a hooker or a meth head.

My wife is my backbone and when it's family time with the misses it's all about us and that is sacred.

We weren't four days into the trip when I get a call from my bondsman Jason.

Mike "Hello"

Jason "Hey Mike, it's Jason"

Mike "I told you not to bother me"

Jason "I know, but I have a problem"

Mike "When do you ever call me with a solution?"

Jason "Mike, I'm serious, I just got a call from your cousin Chepa"

I knew it was going to be about her fuck up grandson and my cousin Chris.

Mike "Ya...My cousin Chepa called you, and?"

Jason "Your cousin Chris is in Commerce County Prison, he needs to get bailed out, the bond is for $10,000"

Mike "Listen, we shouldn't be bonding out family members, especially fuck ups like Chris, if he doesn't show up to court, guess who'll have to go get him Jason? Ya, you're right, me"

Jason "come on Mike, this is easy, having you as the stick to this carrot will insure he shows up to court, won't it?"

Jason obviously didn't know Cousin Chris.

Mike "This is a bad Idea but I'll let you make the call"

Jason "I'll handle it, don't worry, see you when you get back"

Mike "OK, see you when I get back"

I went about having a great vacation, but the whole time I had a nagging feeling about Cousin Chris getting bonded out and hitting the streets.

Sure enough, like clockwork, old faithful and the sun rising, Jason gets a forfeiture of bail in the case of Cousin Chris, who failed to appear in court for his drug arrest.

GREAT!!! Some people never miss an opportunity to just simply fuck up in life one more time, but this time there are family connections at stake.

So I get in my car and go to Mary, Chris's moms house, I tell her what's going on and that I have to look around, she says Chris isn't here but I am welcome to do my job and look around.

I needed to be respectful and I was, trust me, everything was embarrassing and uncomfortable about it.

Somehow Grandma Chepa found out I was at her daughters house and blew a call in as I was about to leave.

Mary "Yes, oh hi Mom, yes I'll put him on the phone, Mike its Chepa, she wants to talk to you"

Mike "Yes Hello"

Chepa "Mike you are really piece of shit, how can you go looking for your own flesh and blood?"

Mike "Listen to me, Chris needs to go to court, it is better I bring him in then a stranger"

Chepa "You really are a piece of scumbag shit you know that? Chris needs our help and you don't give a shit"

Mike "I am trying to help, have him meet me at the house and I'll take him in"

Chepa "Fuck you, you asshole, Help you? You need to be beaten with a rusty pipe"

Mike "Listen to me you crazy old bat, it's either going to be me or it is going to be me, but I am going to catch Chris whether you help me or not.

He broke the law, he's been fucked up for a long time, this could actually help him"

Chepa "Help him? You were always a piece of shit motherfucker…"

Mike "You are an Idiot, good bye"

I knew that Chepa was hiding him now, she made it really clear. People can be pretty see through sometimes, so I headed over to her house.

I called the local sheriff's department and asked for backup, there was going to be trouble when I tried to enter Chepas house, who was I kidding? There already was trouble.

I got dragged into doing a bounty on family, it was escalating and now I had to search another member's house, Chris you piece of shit fuck up, how could you put me in this situation?

Luckily the sheriff's dispatch sent a cruiser out within the hour, which I met outside.

I told them the whole story and they walked with me right up to the front door.

I rang the doorbell, Chepa took a few minutes to answer, but when she did she wouldn't stop cussing me out.

I attempted to ask her nicely to let me in and search the premises, but she was belligerent.

I asked my accompanying officers to talk to her, which did the trick and she finally opened the door and I stepped inside.

Chepa came up to me and threatened to hit me, I warned her that if she touched me I would press assault charges, which was enough to yank her chain in the presence of John Q Law and she calmed down enough for me to finish my search.

I could tell Chris had been sleeping there, but he probably slipped out the back when the cruiser pulled up.

Dear Chepa answered my good night with another juicy fuck you. I thanked the officers for their assistance and headed off to look for Chris, I had a few Ideas of where he could be.

I wasn't a mile down the road when I got a call on my private phone.

Mike "Hello"

Chris "Ha ha ha Mike you piece of shit, you thought you could

63

catch me? You fucking retard, this is my town hommie, I slip and slide in and out and you ain't never going to catch me. But what I wanted to tell you is that everyone in the family knows you're a piece of shit lowlife scumbag for coming after a family member, you ain't ever going to be able to live this down".

Chris didn't sound worried or stressed in the least, he actually sounded really pleased with himself, and confident enough to try and taunt me.

Mike "Listen to me and listen good you world class fuck up, I never cared what anyone thought of me, I don't care now and I won't care tomorrow, You put yourself in this situation and I am going to catch you, this isn't personal, this is now business"
The truth is that I don't give a shit, I don't have any favoritism when it comes to a bounty placed in front of me, if you need arresting I will catch you, period.

Chris "Good luck with your business puto"

Mike "You know I'm going to catch you, you can count on it, walk that to your weed dealer buddies, put it in your hash pipe and smoke it". Chris just hung up.

I started looking around, different places where Chris was known to hang out.

I remembered there is this strip joint off of 80th and Federal in Aravada called Saturday's, Chris use to like to hang out there, flash his cash, stare at titties and get a lap dance.

I drove over there looking for this stripper I knew who went by the name Secret, she knew Chris too and I had an idea.

I told her that he was in trouble and asked if she would help me, she said she would.

I told her if Chris showed up, she was to call me, wait until I answered, give me a few seconds and then hang up, that would be our sign that Chris was in the club.

A day goes by, I exhausted every avenue and now it was just a question of waiting until a lead appeared.

I got home early, around 5pm, had something to eat and started to unwind when the phone rings, I answered it and there was just loud music and then click, the call got disconnected.

Secret! She came through (That's one stripper whose name

64

definitely fit) I grabbed my coat and ran out the door, heading over to Saturday's.

I walked in and headed to the stage, I think Rod Stewart's "Hot Legs" was blasting through the PA system and this Asian chick had her ass up against the silver post on the stripper stage.

Sure enough, front and center was that fat sack of shit Chris, making it rain all up in the club like the wanna be pimp he would like the world to think he is.

I walked up behind him, a friend of his caught a glimpse of me as I was walking up behind Chris and gave him an elbow in the ribs.

Once Chris turned to him, he nodded in my direction, Chris turned around and saw me.

I shouted over the noise "get up" I wasn't playing around.

Chris "Do you have any idea who I am?"

Mike "I don't care who you think you are, start walking or I'll bust you right here in front of everyone"

A bouncer saw that there was some tension between two patrons and walked over to calm things down.

He knew Chris, like I said my Cousin had been spending money at this joint and they must have really liked his business.

Bouncer "What is the problem here?"

Mike "I have a warrant for his arrest"

Bouncer "Not in my club"

I don't know if he didn't want the arrest to occur on the premises or he was trying to protect Chris, but luckily for everyone Chris started walking towards the front door.

I grabbed his shirt above his right shoulder with my left hand from behind and followed him outside, I had a feeling Chris was going to make a run for it or start something so I was cocked and ready.

Just as we got outside Chris turned to swing at me, I ducked his left hook and it was on.

We were bobbing, weaving, punching, kicking, swearing etc…but it was one on one and I was holding my own, Chris wanted to punish me, but I wasn't going to let that happen.

All of a sudden one of his buddies got in on the action, this prick tried to take a swing at me, but I was quick and grabbed him by the throat, forced him on the ground and started to squeeze, then backed off.

I left this dumb ass on the ground coughing and gagging and went right back at Chris.

This time I pulled out the cuffs, managed to cuff one hand mid fight, pulled the hand up which caused pressure on Chris's shoulder and forced him to the ground.
I applied all 230lb of my weight on his back and there was nowhere to go.

All of my adrenalin was pumping double time, and with that came some extra gorilla strength which allowed me to grab his other wrist and cuff it behind his back.

I got his punk ass up off the concrete and led him to the front passenger side of the vehicle.

I closed the door after him and went around to get into the driver's seat when I saw Chris lunging forward and attempting to open the car door with his cuffed hands behind his back.

I got in the car and said "you idiot, it's locked, I had the vehicle child proofed just for Idiots like you"

We headed off towards Adams County Jail, the whole time Chris was popping off, playing the angry card, the hurt card, the "blood is thicker than water" card etc... I was playing the "Shut the fuck up" card, the "I don't give a shit" card, and the "you brought this on yourself" card.

Somehow one of Chris's buddies over at Saturday's saw what happened and called Chepa, because she was at the Adams County Jail before we got there.

I got him out of the car and we started up the ramp towards the entry room.

Chris took one look at his grandma coming towards us and starts getting out of control, so much so that he lurches forward and ran smack dab into the wall, then hit the ground like a sack of laundry.

What came out of Chepas mouth earlier wasn't pleasant by any stretch of the imagination, but what was coming out of her mouth now made her previous comments sound like a lullaby you sing to a child before bedtime.

Too late, Chris was at the jail and no amount of running at the mouth was going to change that.

I got Chris up and we walked into the Jail processing room. Officer DeMarco heard all of the commotion and came to see what all the racket was about.

I gave him the short and concise version of things and he instructed Chepa to leave the premises, she did, loudly but left none the less. I have never seen her since, nor do I care to see her.

Officer DeMarco "Your own cousin, wow, now I have seen it all. I have seen family members drop family members off attempting to do the right thing, but physically arrest a family member, this is a first"

Mike "If any other family member bonds with anyone I am working with and jumps bail, you may see me again"

Chris got 3 year in prison, he served 1 year and was released. The day he got out I got a call from him.

Chris "I an coming for you Mike, I am going to fuck you up for getting me locked up"

Mike "I didn't get caught with the drugs or selling them dumb ass, you did that, and hey! You've been to my house, come by anytime you like, I have another ass whooping chambered for you when you get here"

I have not seen or heard from that idiot since.

12. CBH REALITY CHECK

All things in the universe can be characterized in a very simplistic way, as a combination of two ingredients, which in essence sum up their nature.

There are obviously many layers or facets to anything, but for the purpose of a quick summary, it is possible to lump them all into two basic characteristics.

The sum of those two characteristics can then be distilled into a conclusion.

For example, I have a friend who is a most amazing and gifted carpenter.

He has the ability to join two pieces of wood in a joint and line up the grain so perfectly, that when you look at the final piece it would appear that the tree grew at a 90 degree angle.

At the same time, he has a complete lack of people skills and is incapable of providing his clients with a progress report.

Considering the large ticket prices he charges for his work, the often missing progress reports and the fact that he doesn't return calls in a timely fashion, does not give his high end clientele the peace of mind they feel they are paying for.

As a result, the end product does not compensate for the stress caused during the fabrication, and therefore future recommendations magically never appear.

In the end, even though the end result is outstanding, he is always pressed for work and broke.

All of the above can be distilled into an equation comprised of his two basic characteristics, with a final conclusion which would look something like this;

A Brilliant Individual + A serious lack of people skills = A Tragedy. You can do this to almost anyone in your own life or anyone you meet.

For example; A smart person + A good Heart = A safe individual or A smart person + A bad heart = A dangerous individual or A stupid person + A bad heart = A disaster waiting to happen etc etc...

The world we live in today has added another element to this equation which did not exist in previous generations, and that is the inflated self-esteem characteristic.

We have bombarded a whole generation with ideas like "you can be anything you want be" or Nike's "Just Do It" and "you are amazing, unique and there is no one like you" to the point of super charging them into a massive sense of entitlement.

This probably wouldn't be so bad if it wasn't for the glass like fragility of this super charged self-esteem, especially when it came to a head on collision with rock hard reality.

Case in point, I get a call from Mike at 10pm on a Tuesday.

Mike "Hey Amit, what are you doing" There was that familiar sound of satisfaction in his voice.

Me "Watching the tube and petting the cat, where are you?"

Mike "Dude, I'm driving back home from the Denver County Jail" My initial impression was not wrong, Mike was pleased with himself.

Me "Who did you catch this time?"

Mike "Do you remember about 3 weeks ago I told you I was looking for this fugitive with serious gang affiliations?"

Me "No, this is the first I am hearing about it!"

Mike "Really! I was sure I mentioned it"

Me "No, not a word, this sounds a cut above your usual crack heads" Mike started to laugh.

Mike "I don't get a lot of these types of cases, you're right, Jesus Herrera Ramos was a major distributor for _____ in Denver. (Gang name cannot be mentioned due to the possibility of reprisal)

I got the no hold bond from a new bondsman in Aurora.

When I picked up the file I could see he had gang tattoos, not your regular street or parlor stuff, but real symbolic markings.

One stood out, a black palm on the upper part of his chest.

I wasn't a hundred percent sure what gang he was with, so I took the file to a friend in law enforcement, and he clued me in.

I knew a few things immediately, the most important being when I did find him I needed to get him off the street and into my vehicle as fast as possible. A sloppy arrest that took too long on the street would expose me to his gang and the possibility of their fatal reaction.

So I started off being real careful, parking my car a few blocks away from specific places mentioned in his file and scoping them out on foot.

There were a few addresses in Westminster that ended up being apartment complexes.

I placed a wanted add with the promise of a reward at one of the apartment complexes, a simple black and white with my number, you never know what they may lead to.

This process went on for a week, but there was no sign or wind of Ramos.

I was still looking for other fugitives while working the Ramos case, but from time to time I would pop in on these places, look around and ask residence some questions, but there was nothing. After about 10 days I got a call on my cell phone from a private number, the voice on the line had a pronounced Latino accent.

Mike "Hello"

Voice "You looking for me?"

Mike "Who is this?"

Voice "Jesus"

Mike "Ya, I'm looking for you"

Voice "Do you know who I am?"

Mike "I don't care who you think you are"

Voice "I will be seeing you soon enough" then the line went dead. Ramos was trying to spook me or play head games, I wasn't going to stop looking for him, I just needed to be careful, the way I had been all along.

I got the feeling I was being watched whenever I went looking for him in Westminster, especially in those apartment complexes.

I needed a little bit more information about Ramos, something wasn't quite right.

Even though he was wanted for drug offenses, he didn't appear to be a regular street pusher, so I went back to the courthouse to look at his previous bond cosigner.

On the previous bond was the name Edward Ortega and a number. I called Edward and made an appointment to meet with him.

70

Edward was a truthful kind of guy, he seemed to want to help get Ramos, probably the product of losing his bail money.

He told me that Ramos had connections to some high end clients, pointing out a private Doctors office complex where he believed Ramos sold some of his high quality Heroin.

It was Edwards's belief that Ramos's people placed him in that position to connect him to their clientele.

Edward told me that Ramos did not have a vehicle, he took the bus and walked a lot, preferring to blend in to his surroundings as a way of going under the radar.

I went to the medical office complex Edward had pointed out, looked around then sat back in my vehicle with binoculars for a few hours, but I couldn't see anything out of the ordinary.

At 5pm my phone rang, it was Ramos.

Mike "Hello"

Ramos "You are getting close but not close enough" he hung up.

He obviously saw me at the medical complex, or someone close to him did, I was sure I was being cautious but he was still making me out.

I pride myself on getting the upper hand and springing the surprise catch on my fugitives, but Ramos was beating me at my own game. I needed to blend in even more and really watch my back.

I decided that the visibility of day light was working in his favor and switched my searches to the evening and the cover of dark.

I was about to leave the house this evening when my wife Sonya offered to accompany me.

Having her with me helps passes the time on a long steak out, and another set of eyeballs casing a place comes in real handy.

If I found Ramos I needed to speed up the arrest time, having Sonya drive the vehicle while I set out on foot or back me up with a Taser or just having my back would be safer and faster.

We set out for the apartment complex in Westminster, I was a little hungry so we decided to pick something up at the Burger King off of W 104th.

We weren't in the parking lot for more than a minute when all of a sudden Edward walked up to the car.

Edward "Mike, what are you doing here?"

71

Mike "Oh, just grabbing a bite to eat" Damn, I was getting made by everyone and anyone, what was I supposed to do, dress up as a fire hydrant?

Edward "Listen, there's another place you need to check out, Ramos gets his stuff at the market across the street, if you want I can go there and give you a call if I see him?" I didn't want Edward getting that close to the case.

Mike "Listen Edward, thanks for the help, but let me handle this, ok?"

Edward "Sure, no problem"

Mike "I don't want you anywhere near Ramos when I catch him, it's just healthier, you understand"

Edward "Ya, I get it"

Mike "I'll go check the market out, thanks for your help"

Me and Sonya finished off our burgers and headed for the parking lot of the Super Scooper.

It was getting dark, and my Plymouth was blending in with the other shoppers vehicles perfectly.

We sat and just scoped out the entrance to the apartment complex, whilst keeping an eye on the comers and goer's at the market.

At around 7pm I caught a glimpse of a man that fit Ramos's description walking with a girl across the parking lot.

I told Sonya, to get behind the wheel while I went and grabbed my gear from the trunk, then went and sat in the drivers front passengers seat.

Looking into the binoculars it appeared to be Ramos, but I had to follow him into the store to make a positive ID.

As soon as Ramos stepped into the Super Scooper, I had Sonya drop me off as close to the entrance as possible.

She was to then park the car and keep an eye on the front entrance while I stepped inside.

I walked into the entrance and started scanning from side to side for Ramos.

I saw him with a hand basket walking towards the front so I followed.

Sonya stepped out of the car and walked to the entrance where she could see him and his girlfriend at the front of the store, and she

72

walked towards the checkout lines.

I was now 10 feet behind him, walking slowly and gaining fast.

Ramos and his girlfriend stepped into the checkout line, he looked back for some reason and caught a glimpse of me, and that's when I pounced.

His girlfriend tried to reach me but Sonya had my back and blocked her.

Ramos was putting up a struggle, but he was a skinny weak 5ft 5" little guy, and I had him bent over the checkout counter from behind, my left hand was clutching the back of his neck forcing his head down and I was twisting his right arm behind his back.

He was swearing in a mix of Spanish and English as well as asking other shoppers for help.

I didn't quite have him under control, I was trying to secure the cuffs on his right hand all the while my chain and badge were dangling from my neck.

Mike "Listen to me you little mother fucker, give me your other hand or I will break your arm, give it to me now!!!"

Ramos "Help, help…."

The store manager a white lady in her 40's appeared and started shouting at me "What are you doing? Let this man go, I am calling the Police"

Mike "The badge hanging from my neck says I am a bounty hunter, now back off"

Store Manager "You can't do this in my store"

Mike "Back off and watch me"

A few shoppers understood what was going on and kept their distance, others were shocked and they were voicing their opinion, which gave me the feeling things were not going to work in my favor if this went on for too long.

I now had Ramos's face down on the moving conveyer belt, grinding his grimacing face, the checker finally pressed the button that stopped it from moving.

Mike "Last chance, give me your other wrist or I break your arm"

Ramos moved his left arm behind his back, I grabbed his cuffed wrist and yanked it up towards his left and cuffed them together. Sonya handed me the leg irons which went on in a flash and we

73

headed quickly towards the exit.

Sonya ran ahead and pulled the vehicle up to the front, she opened the drivers front passenger door and I grabbed Ramos by the seat of his pants and threw him in head first.

I quickly ran to the driver's seat got in while Sonya got in the back. Ramos's face was right up against the stick shift, and he was swearing up a storm.

Mike "Listen asshole, keep shouting and I will impale your throat on the stick shift, now shut up"

I needed to get out of that parking lot as soon as possible, I propped Ramos up in his seat and handed the Taser to Sonya.

Mike "Keep it pointed at him at all times, if he gets out of control hit the juice and don't stop Tasing him.

I headed down the road towards the Denver County Jail, Ramos had calmed down a bit but he was still talking mad shit and threatening me.

I turned to my right and took a look at him, he was a kid, the file said he was 22 but he looked 18.

Where was all this self-confidence coming from? He was a little punk, someone had pumped his little ego up or maybe he had seen one too many re-runs of Scarface.

Ramos "When I get out, first thing I do, I kill you, If I don't get out my people will kill your whole family, in my country I kill you in the middle of the street and kick your head in gutter puto"

Mike "Listen to me Ramos, you know what you are?" I had his attention.

Ramos "What you say?"

Mike "Do you know what you are?"

Ramos "What?"

Mike "You are expendable"

Ramos "What is mean, Expendable?"

Mike "It means that your big gang, that one you think will kill people for you, that you think cares about you, that you believe will spend money on lawyers to get you out, they won't lift a finger to help you. You want to know why?"

Ramos "Why?"

Mike "Because once you are behind bars, they will send another kid with dreams of making money to do your job, to take your place while you rot in jail"

Ramos "You are wrong"

Mike "Reality check vato, everyday our prisons get filled with young guys like you, who do the big work for their drug gangs. You are not that special, you are not that powerful even in your own gang.

They let you believe that you are, but once you are caught and are in prison you are nothing. Another thing, you are not an American citizen so once you serve your time, you will get deported back to your country, you are now 22, by the time you get out you will probably be in your 30's, no money, no family, no wife, nothing, nada"

"Your gang, your so called "Familia" are going to let you sit and they will not risk anything in order to get revenge for a little soldier like you. Who do you think they are going to kill for you? The judge? The prison guards? The officer that arrested you? They aren't going to do shit, wake up"

I could hear the little wheels in Ramos's head turning, his eyes were moving from side to side, he knew that he was going away and that it was going to cost him big time.

His massively inflated ego that was a product of his gangs false nurturing just got dented by a reality check, and there were more to come.

Me "Mike, Sonya went along for this one? She wasn't scared?

Mike "She was nervous, but she has my back and never loses her cool, she's been out with me before many times and knows what to do, I can trust her"

Me "She's a good woman Mike"

Mike "Yes sir"

Me "Mike, the kid didn't get into your head? I mean all that talk about getting back at you"

Mike "I have to be cautious that's all, but I can't stop doing my job because some little punk gang member threatens me, no matter who he is" Mike was starting to sound tired, the adrenaline high was probably starting to wear off.

Me "Are you home yet?"

Mike "I'm lying on the couch in the living room"

Me "OK Mike I'll let you go, get some sleep and say hi to Sonya from me".

Mike "I will, good night".

13. OF MICE AND METH

"Hey! That's not fair" How many times have you heard someone say that either to you, a friend, a loved one, on TV, on the floor of congress? Etc…

Maybe it was your kid that didn't like your house rules, well guess what son? My house my rules, this is not a democracy, and when you turn 18 you may have your own place and dictate your rules.

Or maybe you saw a fight on Showtime or the UFC, and the fighter that you thought was winning lost a judge's decision, it happens all the time, fighting is not fair, when a fighter finishes a fight they make it fair by winning.

Life itself is not fair, the strong will beat the weak, a baby gazelle has been known to get devoured seconds after entering this world by a lion in the savannah, a massive black hole in the middle of space will swallow a whole galaxy without a tear being shed and money may buy you justice sometimes.

Is any of this fair? Hell no! But to be aware of it is half of the way to navigating your own justice in this world.

Bounty hunting is no different, it is not a fair game, in fact it isn't a game at all.

There is a "hunt", a cat and mouse or a fox hunt between the bounty hunter and the fugitive, but in the final moments of the catch it is not a fair fight with rules and a sanctioning body, there are no judges on the field to enter a ruling or penalize a player.

It is about the catch, plain and simple and a good bounty hunter will have enough tenacity to finish the job, get his man or maybe it's time to find another line of employment.

I didn't hear from Mike in about four days, it was a Monday and I figured that he had probably been relaxing over the weekend, so I gave him a call just to touch base.

Me "Hey Mike, how was your weekend?"
Mike "Oh, nothing special, we were home"
Me "Needed some time to decompress?"
Mike "More like lick some wounds"
Me "Why? Something happened?"
Mike "Oh boy did something happen"

Me "Do tell", Mike sounded tired, his voice was a bit raspy, but there was that hint of satisfaction that I have become so familiar with.

Mike "I got the paperwork on this No Bond case, for this guy in Lakewood"

Me "What's a no Bond?"

Mike "That's when an individual gets bonded out and hits the streets, but he doesn't show up for his court date, so the judge just says pick him up and then he sits in jail until his trial"

So I have a no bond on this guy Curtis "Kirk" Winston, white guy, 48 years old, 5ft 9" and in the description I see 215lb.

Usually guys with that ratio of height to body weight are fat, but from the picture I see that Kirk is ripped.

He lived up in a part of Lakewood that has large properties, big parcels of land, so I figures this guy was farm and country strong.

I have come across the type before, cowboy boots, cowboy hat, been bailing hay since he could walk, but now all of that property conceals an occasional meth cook, smack dab in the middle of the greater Denver area.

I went to his house Thursday morning to case the place.

The house was as I suspected on a huge parcel of land, and there were several structures on it, including a classic red barn large enough to house 4 large tractors, I am not kidding you this thing was huge.

I drove around looking for Kirks vehicle, but it was nowhere to be found.

I made a drive around the property and I located his vehicle on the next street over.

What Kirk was doing was parking his car next to the wall that ran around his property but clear on the other side, then jumping his own wall and walking home across the grounds, so as to give the impression that he is not there, very clever.

So I went back to the entrance to the property, which offered me a better view through a pair of binoculars and just sat and waited.

I kept a gaze going from 10am to about 4pm and that's when he finally emerged, walking out of the front door and right into the barn.

78

The thing about good bounty hunting is to know when to just lay low and wait, it can be boring sitting for hours waiting for something to happen, but when it's time to act you go from zero to 100 pretty quickly.

You have to couple the waiting with a good element of surprise, and then the catch becomes smoother, but even then it is not always the case.

Kirk walked through the front door of the barn, the side of the barn had the classic double giant wooden doors which are closed from the inside with a 2 by 4, and a back door which I had seen earlier.

I got out of my car and headed to the back of the barn, hoping to surprise Kirk and spring the catch.

The back door was open and I slipped in easily, then barricaded it behind me so that no one could come in or out.

I heard noises from the front of the barn and headed towards them.

The main floor of the barn was empty, just a huge dirt floor, there were piles of hay, equipment and pretty much all the elements you'd expect to find on a Hollywood barn set.

As I walked across the main floor, the noises stopped and I froze using all of my senses to figure out where Kirk could be hiding.

All of a sudden I hear a shout, like a cross between a highlander war cry and a grunting pig directly in front of me, and out of the shadows came kirk charging at me with a pitch fork.

My adrenaline was already pumping, but seeing pitch fork wielding Kirk probably caused my Adrenal glands to dump the last of its stores, and I just leaped out of the way hitting the dirt and springing back to my feet, huffing and puffing.

Kirk was on the other side of the barn now, and I caught my first glimpse of him in the dimly lit barn.

Kirk was huge, you don't see 48 year olds like this every day, he had a massive thick physique.

He wasn't just country strong, but he probably spent some time lifting weights or power lifting or just plain bench pressing anvils.

He was just standing with the pitch fork in his hands looking at me.

That's when I said "Kirk, you're coming with me"

79

Kirk just stood in silence.

Mike "We can do this the easy way or we can do this the hard way, but either way you will be coming with me"

Kirk took the pitch fork and stuck the three prongs into the ground, almost as if he was drawing a line in the sand, a line he was daring me to cross.

Kirk "you are going to have to come and get me"

Mike "OK then, the hard way".

Kirk "Time to dance"

Mike "Let's dance"

What Kirk did next was kind of unexpected, he pulled the pitch fork out of the ground and said "Let me put this away" as if he was setting the battle ground for a fair fight.

When he turned to the side of the barn to put his "prized pitch fork" away I pounced, grabbing his shirt.

Kirk tried to spin around and get his hands on me, he managed to get a grip of my jacket in an attempt to wrestle himself free, and create distance.

I threw a right that landed square on his chin, but it had no effect and now he was trying to hit me with his free hand, but nothing landed clean, just a few slapping shots to the top of my head which knocked my baseball cap off.

We broke away from each other and started to trade punches, I landed some really clean shots but Kirk wouldn't go down.

Thinking back on the exchange, he must have been using his home cooked meth because he wasn't just strong but resilient and frantic, and he broke into a greasy sweat within seconds of our fight.

I was starting to feel that Kirk was not going to slow down and I didn't like the thought of me getting my ass kicked in a barn, with the possibility of never being seen again.

I grabbed the can of mace on my belt and hit him directly in the face, he backed up, turned and tried to move away.

I was on him again from behind, this time unloading the can into his nose and eyes and I didn't stop pulling the trigger on that can.

The mace was flying everywhere and I got a dose of the fumes as well.

My eyes were watering up, I was coughing and I had a scratchy feeling in the back of my throat.

But Kirks experience was worse, there was snot coming from his
nose, he was coughing and spitting.

There's a line in the Johnny Cash song "A boy Named Sue" that goes "we were punchin' and a gougin' in the mud and the blood and the beer", which was exactly what was going down in Kirks barn with the added bonus of mace, minus the beer.

Now the tide was turning, or at least I thought it was, Kirk was blind swinging and missing.

I could punch him at will, and I hit him clean with all of my power
to the jaw and upside the head, but to my surprise he was such a shit brick house that he wouldn't go down.

There is a saying that my pops had drummed into my head, when it comes to fighting "chop the tree" and it will fall.

In boxing that means hit the body and the head will follow, but I wasn't going for any body shots with Kirk, I kicked the inside of his right leg and he finally went down.

I pushed him on his belly and jumped on his back, grabbing one arm with both hands in an attempt to cuff him, but he was so strong that he managed to spin around on to his back and free his hand. I was still on him when I turned and just grabbed him by the nuts and squeezed as hard as I could.

If there was a way to start off a fight with that move I would do it every time, because that finally got him screaming for dear life. Mike "Give me your hand, right now!!! Give it to me or it will get worse"

Kirk "You mother fucker, agggggghhhhhhh….."

Mike "I told you Kirk, you ain't going nowhere".

Kirk put up his hand and I cuffed it with my left hand, all the while keeping an Iron grip on his nuts.

Once I had the one wrist cuffed, I pulled it towards his side then rolled him over to his back, which forced me to let go of my Iron Grip.

I was sitting on the middle of his back, holding the one cuffed wrist.

Mike "Give me your other wrist"

Kirk still had some fight in him, and he wouldn't give the other wrist up.

I pulled the cuffed wrist up towards the back which caused him pain and repeated the request, this time he complied and I cuffed them together.

Kirk was coughing and groaning from the battle and the mace. The adrenaline was starting to fade and I began to feel the fatigue of the last 10 minutes of battle.

Just because you cuff a fugitive does not mean your struggle is over.

I now had to get him out of the barn, off the property, into my car and to the jail.

I got Kirk to his feet, his eyes were shut from all of the mace I had hit them with.

This fool couldn't hit me with a punch to save his life once I maced him, but he managed to gauge the distance between us when he came off the floor, and kicked me in the shin with his steel toe cowboy boot.

That kick hit the mark, it felt like someone had cracked me with a Louisville slugger and I swung a punch right into kirks face.

Mike "You mother fucker, we can do this the easy way or the hard way, your choice again, get up and walk to my car or I will drag you across the ground, what's it going to be?"

Kirk "If you hadn't maced me, if this was a fair fight I would have killed you, you sack of shit"

Mike "This ain't no fair fight, I told you, you were coming with me, now start walking"

We made it to the front of the barn, I tried the door handle but it was closed.

Mike "Where is the key?"

Kirk "I don't know"

I patted him down, and there was no key, we must have lost it while we were dancing on the barn floor.

Mike "Listen, tell me how you locked this door"

Kirk "Figure it out yourself"

I simply lost my patients, I was done with this guy's bullshit, so I positioned Kirk in front of the door, took a few steps back and charged at him like an NFL tackle, crashing through the door and

82

into the outside.

His family was there, a couple of young kids and his wife.

I shouted "Stand back" and we headed down towards the front of the house and down the drive way to my car.

I propped Kirk against the car, then went to the trunk to get a rag and water to clean the mace from his face, and try and wash some of it out of my own throat as well.

I did my best, but he was maced pretty good.

A few people had gathered in the street and maybe one of them had called the cops, because a cruiser came by with two Lakewood officers.

They stepped outside the cruiser and came around the front of my vehicle.

Officer "What do we have here"

Mike pointing to his badge "An arrest officer"

Officer "Who is that?"

Mike "Curtis Winston sir"

Officer "Kirk? You managed to catch a 1000lb gorilla, we know this guy, he's one tough cowboy, good Job"

The officers helped me get Kirk into the car, he was still struggling but once we were in the car it was off to Arapahoe County Jail.

Kirk "You are one son of a bitch"

Mike "Ya, now you know and if I have to come back here again, we'll do this again"

Kirk "Hey man, I am having a hard time breathing, oh shit I think I'm going to throw up, you've got to let me out, get me some water man" the whole time Kirk was coughing and snot was running down his nose, the residual effect of a can of mace being unloaded into his face.

The last thing I wanted was for Kirk to asphyxiate in my vehicle or puke.

I pulled over, exited the vehicle and walked over to the driver's passenger side.

I went to open the door and Kirk tried to kick the door open, hitting me in the pelvis, this mother fucker was still trying to get away!

83

I slammed the door shut and double timed it to the prison, I didn't want any more trouble and I wasn't taking any more chances.

Once at the Jail, I got Kirk out of my vehicle and walked him up to the entrance, all the while being very cautious of any tricks he may attempt to pull on me at the last minute.

The on duty sheriff took one look at us both and said "someone threw down this afternoon, didn't they?"

We were a mess, clothes torn, Kirks eyes swollen and red from the mace and I was now limping from his shin kick.

The Sherriff walked up to Kirk and started getting some information from him, that's when Kirk repeated his earlier statement "If this fucking guy didn't have mace, this would have been a fair fight and I would have kicked his ass...."

The Sheriff looked at Kirk and said "This is not a fair fight, a street fight never is", dear Kirk's ego was having a hard time dealing with his ass whooping and inevitable incarceration.
I chuckled to myself and headed out the door, man did I need a shower.

When I finally got home, I limped through the front door where my wife met me, she knows what I do and doesn't baby me.

She just gave me that look, the one that says "It looks like you had a rough day at the office".

Me "so how's the leg?"

Mike "I had it X-Rayed today, it's not broken but I am not running a marathon any time soon, I'll take it easy this week"

14. THE KINGMAN SHUFFLE

When you think of traveling to certain cities, you think about what they are famous for.

For instance, if you think of San Francisco you might think of Ghirardelli chocolates, or if you are in Atlanta you may want to catch some Barbecue. If you're in Philadelphia you might salivate for a Cheese steak or if you're in LA you may want to get some Roscoe's Chicken and Waffles (God knows how such bad food combining got to be such a hit, I don't care if individually each one is delicious, in the name of health and good taste they should never have been placed on the same plate together, but that's just me).

The same can be said for Kingman AZ. except that chance are you didn't go there with a hankering for a now world famous locally spawned food, but rather a junky itch or dealer greed for Meth. Yes folks, Kingman AZ could be considered the Meth capital of the South West.

And to the good folks of Kingman, it may be time to invest some thought in a really tasty salad or sandwich.

A Kingman on Rye with a side of Coleslaw or a Kingman salad with Jerky Chicken may go a long way to improve your reputation. Either that or get a better publicist.

Meth is not just a drug, there is a whole sub culture that goes along with it.

From the individuals that buy the raw materials at the local pharmacies for cooking, the cookers, the distributors, the users and gangs that run Meth in and out of towns in the US, Meth is a phenomena on to itself.

Case in point, I get a call from Mike on Wednesday Morning.

Mike "Hey Amit, what are you doing?" Mikes way of saying good morning.

Me "Good morning Mike, you sound pumped up, a little early to be out chasing hookers again? Don't worry I won't tell the misses" I couldn't resist.

Mike "Hey funny boy, my wife knows I catch those as well.

Listen I'm heading to the car rental agency, I have a Hummer waiting for me"

Me "Why? Did you get in an accident?"

Mike "No, I have a bounty in Arizona, the bondsman is renting me the Hummer"

Me "They've got you going two states over? You're almost close enough to pop in on me for a visit, sounds serious"

Mike "The guy is wanted for a drug offense, probably distribution but I'm not sure, I'm meeting Jason my bondsman at the car rental agency"

Me "Where are you going in Arizona?"

Mike "Kingman, I haven't seen the file yet, I'll know more after I see Jason"

Me "OK Mike, go get'em"

Mike "You know I will"

I didn't hear from Mike all day Wednesday, but at 5:30pm on Thursday my cell phone rang and it was Mike.

Me "Hey Mike, how was Kingman? What's all that noise in the background?" There was a man screaming, I couldn't make out what he was screaming about just the occasional MF'er and SOB, he sounded pissed.

Mike "Amit, I'm in a gas station in Albuquerque, the cussing and screaming you are hearing is from one Aaron Weller my fugitive.

He's in the backseat of the Hummer on his belly, hog tied ankles to wrists behind his back like a mother fucking banana, and if he doesn't calm his jolly green giant ass down, he's going to stay that way all the way to Denver, You hear me Aaron?"

Me "Wait a minute, how long have you had him tied up like that?"

Mike "Since we left Kingman"

I was a little taken back, being tied up in a banana position for that long does not feel like a deep tissue massage at a five star spa, if you know what I mean.

Me "What made you do that? You got into Kingman yesterday, it's now Thursday night, when did you hogtie him"

Mike "When I got off the phone with you yesterday, I headed south on I-25 to Albuquerque, then west on the 40 to Arizona.

I got to Kingman late, I was tired so I took it easy and just found a hotel for the night.

In the morning I got up, went and got breakfast, then headed out

86

to the address we had in the file with Aaron's mug shot in it.

Aaron is a big guy, 6ft 2 around 220lb in his 30's clean shaven, with shoulder length brown hair.

The address was in a neighborhood of modular homes, with walls around the properties.

It's real hot here in Arizona or maybe I'm just not use to this coming from Denver.

I parked my rental just out of sight, and was about to get out of my car in order to take a look around the property, when I saw the front door open.

I sat back and pulled my binoculars out, then followed the man now walking from the front door to a black car parked in the front yard.

The man was carrying a long black object and at first I couldn't see what it was exactly, but once he popped the trunk open I got a better look, it was an AK47.

Now I had to be on my toes, I needed to find the right opportunity to grab this guy without giving him time or the opportunity to gain access to that weapon.

After placing the rifle in the trunk Aaron returned to the house.

I was thinking there is now enough distance between the rifle and Aaron, but if I tried to get him at the house he is sure to have another weapon inside.

Before I could think about my next move, Aaron came out of the house, got in his car and drove off quickly, like he was in a hurry.

I started following him, he ran a red light and I was hanging back close enough to follow him but not enough to give myself away, but I still had to go through the light.

The black vehicle pulled into a gas station so I followed him, even though my tank was full I pulled up to a pump, and pretended to fill up for gas.

Aaron was still in his vehicle, just at another pump on the other side of the station, except he had turned around and was facing the entrance from which we both had entered.

I still went about pretending to fill the Hummer with gas, all the while glancing from time to time at the black vehicle.

All of a sudden the black car started to roll towards the entry way.

The window was rolled down and Aaron was looking directly at the Hummer, I could tell he was looking for the license plate and sizing me up.

Our gazes met, immediately followed by the one glimpse of the Hummers Colorado license plate, and he floored it out of the station. I jumped in the hummer, but in order to follow him, I needed to turn the vehicle around which cost me some time.

By the time I left the station I could only follow in the general direction he had left, there was no clear view of the black vehicle.

So I drove down the road a few blocks as fast as I could, keeping my eyes peeled for the Aarons car, but I couldn't see him.

I was standing at the light a few blocks away and no Aaron, damn! I lost him.

Just then I looked to my right, there was a gas station on the other side of a barren field, and a black car was parked next to a pump.

I wasn't sure it was him, but I took a chance and crossed the field in the Hummer and ended up at the back of the station, and out of site.

I then got out of my vehicle and walked around the station to see if this black car was Aaron's.

Sure enough it was his, the car was still on and it looked like Aaron had stepped into the gas station to pay for gas.

I pulled out my Taser and waited between the pumps for Aaron to appear.

Not a minute after positioning myself strategically to see but not be seen, out came big Aaron.

He was big alright, but he was soft, pudgy and not the least bit physically imposing a character at all.

I stepped out from behind the pump that concealed me, Taser in hand, pointing it directly at Aarons chest and with force and authority shouted "Get on the ground you big mother fucker, get on the ground now or I will Tase you right in the mother fucking chest, on your knees now!!!"

All I knew is that the last thing I wanted Aaron to do was get to the trunk of his car, and I was going to do everything to prevent that.

There were people staring at us now, one car just took off and a few folks who were already walking to the gas store were spooked enough to run inside.

Aaron was not the athletic running type who would have attempted to challenge me to a game of catch or hide and seek.

Aaron got down on both knees, I kept the Taser on him the whole time I was walking behind him, where I pulled out my cuffs and cuffed him.

He didn't struggle, I grabbed the chain between the cuffs and walked him to the Hummer, placed him in ankle Irons, got him in the front passengers seat and off we went.

I caught my breath, an AK47 in the hands of a drug fugitive has a tendency to spell ugly.

We were heading towards the 40 when Aaron spoke "Are you taking me to Mojave County Jail?"

Mike "No, you're coming with me to Jefferson County Jail, you know where that is right? That's where you skipped bail, remember?"

Aaron "Do you have any Idea who I am?"

Mike "Let me guess, Frankenstein's mentally retarded little brother?"

Aaron "I am a ranking member of the _____. (The gang name cannot be mentioned due to the possibility of reprisal)

Mike "And your dickhead band of brothers means what to me?"

To be honest, I had never heard of these guys before.

Aaron "It means that we move more Meth than Heisenberg on Breaking Bad, and if I am missing and my people find out that you were the asshole dipshit wetback that grabbed me, you are going to be dead, and dead quick" I have heard threats like this before, everyone is connected, everyone is "El Chapo" Guzman's favorite nephew.

Mike "Oh wow, now I am really scared, but guess what Tinny Tim, that won't change shit, you are going back to Colorado with me, so get comfortable"

No sooner than I had finished uttering those words, Aaron lifted his legs and pushed the steering wheel, forcing the hummer into the guard rail.

I grabbed the wheel with my left hand firmly, attempting to steady the car, and smacked Aaron as hard as I could with hammer fists to the face.

I managed to pull the Hummer over to the right and slow down, then I brought it to a full stop by the side of the road.

Mike "You want to fuck around and play games, let's fuck around"

I stepped out of the car, pulled Aaron out of the front by the side of the road.

I kicked the back of his knees from behind forcing him to his knees, then on to his belly.

Mike "You want to play games?"

Aaron "You mother fucker, wait until I get out of these cuffs, I am going to kill you…"

Mike "The only thing you will be killing is time in jail with one of your gang girlfriends"

I grabbed a piece of chain from the trunk of the car, then paddle locked it to his feet and joined it to his handcuffs, tightening the distance between the two as much as possible.

In essence, Big Bad Aaron was now looking more and more like a banana on the side of the I-40.

I don't know how I picked him up, but I got him belly down in the back of the Hummer and headed east towards Albuquerque.
So to answer your question Amit, he has been this way for 6 ½ hours, and screaming his head off the whole time".

Me "Maybe he's in pain?"

Mike "That's not what he's screaming about, he's threatening to kill me and shit" I couldn't Imagine having to hear a guy freak out like that for 6 ½ hours.

Hold on Amit, hang on the line, two motor cycle cops just pulled up to the station and they're parked right behind me, I'll leave the phone on so you can hear the exchange" This was going to be interesting.

Officer "What's going on here?"

Mike "Good evening officer, I'm a bounty hunter and this is a fugitive I am transporting to Denver".

Officer "You're a long way from home, by the way, why is he freaking out like that, does he need medical assistance?"

90

Mike "He's being difficult, he shoved my steering wheel and caused me to hit a guard rail"

Officer "I see, the vehicle is scraped up pretty good, do you mind if I take a look at him, someone called and said there was a person freaking out in your vehicle, we just want to make sure everything is alright"

Mike "Be my guest"

I heard the door to the Hummer open, then the officer spoke in an amused tone.

Officer "Hold on, let me call my partner over, Max you've got to see this!" Aaron was silent for a moment and then I heard laughter.

Officer "You've been transporting him like this from Kingman? Ha ha ha ...." The other officer joined in the laughter and I could recognize Mike's laughter joining in the chorus as well.

Officer "You don't mind if we run his ID through the system do you?"

Mike "Not at all"

Mike "Amit, are you catching this"

Me "Yes, every word, this is hilarious"

Mike "He's going to run Aaron's information, keep hanging on the line" Mike's voice had a mischievous sound to it, he was enjoying this I could tell, I couldn't help but laugh out loud myself.

Officer "Mr. Quintana, Aaron Weller has an extradition warrant, which means that we could take him off of your hands right now and hold him until a Jefferson County Sherriff picks him up"

Mike "No thank you, after almost running me off the road, Mr. Weller will be making the bumpy ride home with me, I'm not giving him the easy way out now"

Officer "OK, (Chuckle) I get it, have a safe trip home"

Mike "Officer, one last thing, I'm going to give Mr. Weller here a final chance to calm down and behave himself, or he can make it all the way to Colorado in his current state of comfort". The Officer turned to Aaron.

Officer "You've got a long way to go Mr. Weller"

Mike "What's it going to be Weller? Easy way or the hard way?

Aaron "OK, OK, just let me out of these fucking chains!!!"

Mike "Officer, can you please help me get Aaron out of the

vehicle, I will undo his back ties and then help me transfer him to the front passenger side?"

Officer "Sure thing" For several minutes I could hear them moving Aaron around, but at least he wasn't freaking out anymore.

Mike "Thanks Guys". I could hear the officer's bikes drive away.

Mike "Amit are you still there"

Me "Yes Mike, I caught all of it" once again I couldn't help but laugh.

Mike "Amit, I'll call you after I have this guy locked up, will you be up?"

Me "Call me whenever you're done"

At 4 in the morning my phone rang, it was Mike, and even though I was tired I still wanted to hear what happened.

Mike "Hey Amit, you up?"

Me "I am now, what happened?"

Mike "After we left the gas station I got hungry, so I pulled over at this Mexican Restaurant.

I asked Aaron if he wanted to eat but he was being a dickhead, mouthy and just miserable.

So I just told him that he can sit in a booth with me and watch me pound delicious Mexican food.

Mike "I can't believe you'd give up a perfectly delicious free meal. The next time you'll be able to eat this quality food will be in a few years, I strongly suggest you take advantage of this last opportunity"

My reasoning was finally reaching his otherwise unreasonable brain, and he decided to order something from the menu.

Aaron "How am I supposed to eat my food with my hands tied?"

Mike "Open that huge mouth of yours, you know, the one that wouldn't stay shut from Kingman to Albuquerque, put the Burrito in it and make like a Piranha"

Aaron "You know something, you're a real asshole you know that?"

Mike "Normally I would say to a guy in your position that I'm supposed to be an asshole and that I'm not here to be your friend, but you know what Aaron, from here to Colorado we are going to be friends, in fact we are going to be best friends"

92

Aaron "What makes you think I would want to be your friend"
Mike "A 4ft length of chain that could always turn you back into the banana you were from Kingman to Albuquerque" I smiled and Aaron finally shut up.

We got up to leave and Aaron decided even though his feet were in irons that he wanted to take his slim chances at freedom, and run Cornelius from the planet of the ape's style towards the front door. I grabbed his shirt from behind and said in my most parental voice "Now where do you think you are going?"

Aaron "Fuck you, I'm not going to Colorado"

Mike "Are we really going to have this conversation? Do you really think that after our hot date at the Mexican restaurant and all the trouble I've been through that I was just going to let you go?"

Aaron started to freak out again and get loud inside the restaurant, so I grabbed the bandana from inside his back pocket and shoved it in his mouth, I should have done that back in Arizona.

When we were back in the Hummer he still wouldn't shut up, except that hearing him mumble insults through the rag stuffed in his mouth was at least funny.

We finally pulled up to Jefferson County Jail about 2am, I rang the bell and the officer came out.

When I finally pulled the bandana out of Aaron's mouth the first thing he said to the officer was "This guy is a prick!!!"

Officer "If I had to bring you all the way from Kingman, you'd think that I was a prick too".

My cuffs and ankle Irons needed to be removed, so we stepped into a cell where the officer removed mine and exchange them with their own.

Before I left, Aaron Weller made a body gesture at me something akin to "I'm going to get you", the officer saw that and shoved Weller deeper into the cell.

Me "Aren't you afraid of these guys catching up with you?"

Mike "I can't be scared, it comes with the job man, if I start cherry picking who I catch based on what is safe I won't leave the house"

Me "But don't you think Jason your bondsman could have at least warned you about this guy's gang affiliations?"

Mike "He could have, but that wouldn't have changed a thing, a bounty is a bounty, it's what I do and I love my job".

Me "Mike you know you're nuts, right?"

Mike "Ya, my wife says that, my dad says that, it was only a matter of time before I heard it from you".

15. ATTACK OF THE ZOMBIE CHIHUAHUA

I got up at around 8am on a Saturday, had breakfast and then went to see what's new on Facebook.

Mike had posted a picture of a white two story house with a slanted moss covered roof.

The stairs leading from the front second story porch to the front yard looked rickety, and the roofs drain looked like it was one rain storm away from falling off.

The post underneath the picture read "CRACK SHACKS R US, Come out bitch I know you're in there C.B.H is here to assist you back to jail". Now that was really Mike at his finest, up early on a Saturday and already on the hunt, I smiled and chuckled to myself.

The screen of my phone lit up and started to ring with the familiar QB image taken from Mikes red baseball cap, it was 3:43pm.

Mike "Amit, Amit Holy shit man, you'll never believe what just happened? Is this a good time to talk?" He sounded amped up and out of breath".

Me "Of course Mike, what's going on?" I was already cracking a smile for the second time today on account of Mike.

Mike "Amit, I'm telling you, I just finished arresting the craziest bitch I have ever had to deal with. I struggled with her for 30 minutes in an ally!" That didn't sound like Mike, he usually gets things done faster and more professionally than that.

Mike "You saw the picture I posted this morning right?"

Me "Ya, I did, the one that said Crack Shacks R US" I started to laugh out loud and Mike joined me with a more mischievous version of his usual laughter.

Mike "I got this $3000 bond yesterday for Elizabeth De La Cruz, 29 years old, 5ft 4 and maybe 110lb.

It was pretty simple stuff, your regular garden variety drug offense. The file had the consigner's name and number, so I gave him a call.

It turned out that the cosigner was this Chicano guy who fell in love with Elizabeth and brought her from Mexico to live with him in the states.

He was a real solid guy and the plan was for them to live together for a while and then get married.

Elizabeth got into some serious drugs and the relationship went of the wheels, but not before her fiancé bailed her out.

After he posted bail, Elizabeth left him for some lowlife drug dealer.

I asked the fiancé if he knew her whereabouts and he pointed to the crack shack.

I sat there for 2 hours this morning but there was nothing coming or going.

At around noon the door opened and a man stepped out, I assumed this was her new boyfriend, he got into a car and drove down the road.

I followed him for 6 blocks, the car stopped and the man got out and entered another house which looked better than the crack shack.

I sat and waited, something wasn't right, Elizabeth wasn't in the nice house, that was the dealers nice place, she was back at the crack shack and I could feel it, so I turned around and repositioned myself down the road and out of view.

I waited for about 20 minutes and then the second story door opened, there was Elizabeth and she was lugging 4 large trash bags down the stairs.

There was no time to lose, I rolled the car as close to the house as possible, jumped out of my car as quickly and as inconspicuously as can be, then headed towards the dumpsters on the side of the house.

The side of the house was one great big concrete patch.

I didn't want to engage her until she placed the trash bags in the dumpsters, she is a Heroin addict and I didn't want to get pierced by a used needle from one of the bags.

Once she closed the lids to the trash I pulled out my Taser, came up as close as I could and shouted "Get on the ground now!!!"

Elizabeth tried to run but I fired the Taser into her back and hit the juice.

The 50,000 volts went through her with no effect! Amit, I'm telling you I've never seen anything like it, she should have gone down but she just started to run.

I grabbed her from behind and pulled her to the ground, she started to scream in Spanish "pinchi maricon, pinchi puto" over and over again, growling and grunting.

I tried to force my whole body weight to keep her down, but she kept on flipping and turning like a maniac. Whenever I thought I had her pinned down she managed to escape and get to her feet.

Hold on, I have to take a minute to catch my breath, I'm still exhausted" Mike stopped for a second and I could hear him take a few deep breaths before continuing the story.

He would take a breath then let out a "wow" then catch another breath, he sounded beat but he also sounded as if he had accomplished a monolithic feat.

Mike "Amit, remember I told you the story about the time I went one on one with that drug dealer Sunshine?"

Me "Yes, I remember"

Mike "I'm telling you, this bitch was much stronger, it must have been the mix of Heroin and Meth she was on.

While I was wresting her I was able to catch a glimpse at her arms, there were tracks on both arms, and she also had sores on her face, all the classic signs of a Heroin and Meth addict.

Nothing was slowing her down, I even punched her square right on the chin and that didn't stop her.

She got right back up to her feet and I lunged at her, she anticipated my move and caught me with kick square in the nuts, it hurt like a bitch but I wasn't going to let her get away.

There were cars driving past the house and a few passersby, but for the most part this whole battle went on in a bubble as if we were invisible to the world.

Our fight went on for about 25 minutes, almost the longest I have ever had to go one on one with a fugitive.

All of a sudden a neighbor appeared, he recognized Elizabeth and asked me if I needed help.

At this point I was sitting on top of her chest, trying to figure out a way to get the cuffs on her wrists behind her back.

I shouted at him "Grab her legs" which he did, it took all of his strength to pin them to the ground but that finally turned the tide.

I was able to get a cuff around her wrist, then with the neighbors help roll her over on to her stomach and cuff the other wrist.

The fact that she was in cuffs did not stop her from struggling, attempting to bite me or from screaming and cussing.

I got her to her feet and she kicked me hard in the shin, which hit the mark more powerfully than the swift kick to the nuts I had experienced 5 minutes earlier.

I let out a shout "ouch, you little bitch" then grabbed her cuffs from behind, pulled them up towards her neck, forcing her to move forward or suffer the pain of the pressure on her arms and shoulders.

Even though we were now moving towards the front yard, she was still bouncing up and down trying to get away.

She jumped backwards trying to hit me with her shoulders, which I side stepped and she landed right on her ass.

I got her up and she tried to repeat this process and in one instant almost did a back flip.

I got her into my vehicle and locked the door, she was still screaming and thrashing around.

No sooner had I got her into my car when a Denver Police cruiser showed up.

The officer exited the cruiser and walked up to me gun drawn, his name tag said Woodman. I had my badge hanging from my neck and I turned to talk to the officer.

Mike "It's OK officer Woodman, I have her under control"

Officer Woodman "Who the hell are you?"

Mike "I'm a bounty hunter, I have just arrested this fugitive"

The officer walked up to me, grabbed my Taser and threw it into the bushes.

Officer Woodman "Anyone can buy a badge from a gumball machine, turn around facing the vehicle and place your hands behind your back"

What the hell!!! We are on the same side, what was this cop's problem?

I complied, the last thing you want to do is get on the wrong side of the law in a tense situation such as this.

I know quite a few officers in the Denver area but I didn't know Woodman.

All of a sudden a second cruiser appeared, the driver's side door opened and out came a second officer. I recognized Officer White, he was Woodman's ranking superior.

Officer White walked up to Woodman to try and figure out what was going on.

Officer White "Hey Mike, what happened here?" He asked the question with a hint of humor and a smile.

Mike "I just finished wrestling with that Zombie Chihuahua bitch in the back of my Hummer over there, I mean look at me, does it look like we were dancing or what?"

Officer Woodman "He had a Taser in his front pocket, I tossed it in the bushes"

Officer White "He's a bounty hunter Ned! He's supposed to have a Taser and pepper spray, get him out of those cuffs will you"

Officer Woodman looked real embarrassed, he removed the cuffs and started to apologize.

Mike "It's OK, you were just doing your job, I get it"

Officer White "Would you like us to take Elizabeth in? We were here a few nights ago, we've been at the house every few days but we couldn't catch her"

Mike "I am beat guys, if you took her off my hands I would really appreciate it, I also have to go pick up my wife, we have a birthday to go to and as you can see I really need to clean up".

The Officers got Elizabeth out of the Hummer, she was still freaking out, but they were able to replace my cuffs with theirs and off they went.

Me "Mike where are you now?"

Mike "I am outside of Sonya's work, waiting to pick her up"

Me "So you haven't been home yet, you're still all jacked up from your wrestling match with the Zombie?"

Mike "Yes, man she got me good, my knee hurts, my shin hurts, my right hand knuckles are all scraped up and my brand new Adidas are all scraped up too"

Me "And all of that for $300?"

Mike "Yes, but it was a pretty good workout too" Mike started to laugh and I couldn't help but join him.

Made in the USA
Middletown, DE
30 September 2017